ANSWERS WITHIN

BIBLICAL SOLUTIONS TO LIFE'S TOUGHEST CHALLENGES

RALPH B. LASSITER

WESTBOW
PRESS®
A DIVISION OF THOMAS NELSON
& ZONDERVAN

WestBow Press books may be ordered through booksellers or by contacting:

WestBow Press
A Division of Thomas Nelson & Zondervan
1663 Liberty Drive
Bloomington, IN 47403
www.westbowpress.com
844-714-3454

ISBN: 979-8-3850-3722-3 (sc)
ISBN: 979-8-3850-3723-0 (e)

Library of Congress Control Number: 2024922897

Print information available on the last page.

WestBow Press rev. date: 10/30/2024

DEDICATION

For my wife, Doris, who is my rock
throughout our life journey together.

For my parents, Wright and Ethel, who modeled
faithfulness to the gospel and family.

For my Preaching Brethren, who encourage
my work in kingdom building.

EPIGRAPH

Blessed is the one who perseveres under trial because, having stood the test, that person will receive the crown of life that the Lord has promised to those who love him. – James 1:12

I can do all this through him who gives me strength. – Philippians 4:13

Cast all your anxiety on him because he cares for you. 1 Peter 5:7

For I am the LORD your God who takes hold of your right hand and says to you, Do not fear; I will help you. - Isaiah 41:13

Trust in the LORD with all your heart and lean not on your own understanding;

6 in all your ways submit to him, and he will make your paths straight. Proverbs 3:5-6

CONTENTS

INTRODUCTION

Jesus said in Matthew 16:24, "Whoever wants to be my disciple must deny themselves and take up their cross and follow me." Since the cross was a place of death, taking up your cross implied the death, not of the person, but of the person's desires, wants, and preferences. But the tension between our desires, wants and preferences often challenges our daily walk with Christ.

The Apostle Paul said in 2 Timothy 3:16-17 that *"All Scripture is God-breathed and is useful for teaching, rebuking, correcting and training in righteousness, so that the servant of God may be thoroughly equipped for every good work."* In other words, the Bible has an answer for every challenge.

In the chapters that follow, I will explore what the Bible provides as "teaching, rebuking, correcting and training" to address many of the more common challenges faced by Christians. The concluding chapters focus on the understanding that God will give us the strength and the wisdom to know that "he works all things for our good" including life's challenges. I pray that these reflections will encourage you on your walk with Jesus Christ, our Lord and Savior.

- Ralph B. Lassiter, Sr.

CHAPTER 1

CHOICES AT THE CROSSROADS

Pastor Tim Baker writes, "I remember so clearly my storm chase on May 13th, 2009 of the Kirksville, Missouri tornado. "My chase started with spotting my first tornado near Novinger Missouri, where I played tag with it several times, getting some nice video clips of it, until finally it approached the city limits wrapped in rain. Many cars were at the main crossroad leading into the city, and that is where I turned and stopped to try to spot the tornado again. While sitting there I realized none of the people in the cars around me knew the tornado was only minutes away from them. They simply didn't know.

"I wound down my car window and yelled at people warning them a tornado was heading their way. A few drove away from the storm, but many sat in front of that tornado as it approached. It was rain-wrapped, meaning there was so much rain around the tornado at this point no one could see the tornado, just the rain. After yelling my last warnings, I drove out of its path, where the tornado then moved into the small town and took the life of one person in her home.

"At this point I started to become overly confident, believing I was incapable of making a bad decision. I drove to a road that put me in the path of the tornado one more time, and there I tagged the tornado again, getting within 50 yards of it, it was slightly visible within the rain curtain and looked larger than before it hit the city. I shot some great video as it hit the trees in front of me. It started raining hard at this point, so I decided to break off the chase of this storm since seeing the tornado became impossible.

"So, I headed east to intercept the storm that was building near Kirksville to film the next tornado. "By the time I caught up to this second storm, it was now producing a powerful and deadly tornado where it took two lives. Feeling as though I was in control of everything around me, I decided to cut in front of the tornado to film it as it destroyed buildings near me. The problem was I mistakenly turned onto a dead-end road, where I became trapped in the path of the damaging tornado with no place to go.

"I sat in my car, certain of death at this point. As debris from the tornado pounded my car, I watched large pieces of plywood, siding, and 2X4s flying past me, some of them slamming into my car so hard it shook. Expecting that I wasn't going to survive this, I prayed to God telling Him my life was in His hands. I completely surrendered to God's will and sovereign power. Miraculously I was not killed, I wasn't even injured.

"With the first tornado, many people's lives were in grave danger but they didn't understand what was happening so they didn't grasp the danger. With the second tornado, I knew what was happening, I knew how dangerous the tornado was, but I failed to make good decisions.

"God tells us what is coming in the Bible and we need to seek out this truth, to learn it. Choosing to ignore God's Word doesn't make you safe, it makes you uninformed. Choosing to learn of God's truth still doesn't make us safe by itself, we need to act on it correctly and make the appropriate choices. Then when we surrender to God's Word and act on it wisely, we will find life in Christ and the safety He brings."

Everyone encounters a crossroads - a place of decision-making that has the potential to affect the course of our lives. Your crossroad could be a job decision, a decision about a relationship, sometimes it's a decision about staying or moving to a city or a home; or a decision about remaining in a church or continuing to serve in a church ministry. Those can be difficult or easy decisions, and whether we realize it or not, they can be crossroads moments.

In the sixth chapter of Jeremiah, we read in verses 16 through 19, *"This is what the Lord says: "Stand at the crossroads and look; ask for the ancient paths, ask where the good way is, and walk in it, and you will find rest for your souls. But you said, 'We will not walk in it.' I appointed watchmen over you and said, 'Listen to the sound of the trumpet!' But you said, 'We will not listen.' Therefore hear, you nations; you who are witnesses, observe what will happen to them. Hear, you earth: I am bringing disaster on this people, the fruit of their schemes, because they have not listened to my words and have rejected my law.*

Jeremiah reminds us of a time in Israel's history when Israel was divided into two kingdoms, Israel, the northern kingdom, and Judah, the southern kingdom. This division occurred after the death of King Solomon.

Well, Judah has become complacent in their devotion to God. They wanted prophets and preachers who would tell them what they wanted to hear; someone to tell them that there was no need to change their ways; and that all was well despite their disobedience to God's Holy Word.

But Jeremiah receives a message from God to tell the people of Judah that they are at a crossroads and they have to decide if they will turn to the right and find rest or they can turn in the other direction and experience disaster. So how does God want Judah and us to make the right choice when at a crossroads of life? Based on Jeremiah's writing, I suggest that we should remember a 3-letter word, LAW – which stands for Look, Ask, and Walk.

In verse 16, we are told to stand at the crossroads and to look. In other words, to make the right choices when at a crossroads of life, we first have to recognize that we are at a crossroads. Your crossroad could be a health situation; a career or job decision; a relationship decision; a major buying decision; or even a decision about service to the Lord.

You won't make a good choice if you don't recognize that you are at a crossroads and know that crossroads always offer more than one option. So, when faced with a challenging situation, when you stand at a crossroads, take the time to look – to recognize that the road you take can have long-lasting consequences.

Well, upon recognizing that you are at a crossroads, Jeremiah tells us that we should ASK a question. He says that we should **"ask for the old paths, where the good way is."**

Why should you ask? Just because a certain path or course of action seems right, there is no guarantee that it is right. The Bible says in Proverbs 14:12, *"There is a way that appears to be right, but in the end, it leads to death."*

In other words, they should look to their history and forefathers – the **old paths**, to learn from what God had done previously. One of the old paths is found in the 13th chapter of Genesis where Abram and his nephew Lot are in a new land. Upon their arrival, there was not enough space for both family groups and their herds so they needed to split up. This was a crossroads situation.

Abram gave Lot the first choice and Lot chose the land that looks good to his eyes. He chose land that was near the cities of Sodom and Gomorrah. Abram listened to the Lord who said look and go where I direct you. Lot and his family were infected by the sin of those around him and Abram was blessed.

Unfortunately, when we are more concerned about the popular than the right, the pleasurable instead of the principled, the secular instead of the spiritual, not only do we miss the fact that we are at a crossroads, we make poor choices as did Lot.

The truth is that God's ways are not our ways. In Isaiah 55:8-9 God says, *"For my thoughts are not your thoughts, neither are your ways my ways. As the heavens are higher than the earth, so are my ways higher than your ways and my thoughts than your thoughts."*

When standing at a crossroads in life, none of us can afford to rely upon our understanding. Because of our finite nature, there is no guarantee that our choices are the correct ones. But there is an all-wise, an all-knowing, and an all-loving God who never fails. There is a God who knows everything about us and every situation we find ourselves in. He knows the end from the beginning, and He will lead us in the way that is best for us.

So, when standing at the crossroads of life, how do we know God's way? Well, the best way is to consider the old ways that give glory and honor to God. The old ways as laid out in God's Holy Word.

Psalm 12:6-7 tells us that *"The words of the Lord are pure just like silver."* Paul told Timothy that *"All Scripture is God-breathed and is useful for teaching, rebuking, correcting and training in righteousness, so that the servant of God may be thoroughly equipped for every good work."* (2 Timothy 3:16-17)

So, when you find yourself at the crossroads of life remember that God's Word is the best guide and it never fails. Isaiah 40:8 states *"The grass withers and the flowers fall, but the word of our God endures forever."*

Finally, Jeremiah tells us that after we LOOK and recognize that we're at a crossroads, and having ASKED the Lord for guidance through His Holy Word, we should get to stepping. In other words, to benefit from the **old paths**, God told them to **walk in** them – to *obey* and *follow* God as indicated by His word and His work in days gone by. **Then you will find rest for your souls.**

When you choose to obey the will of God for your life, you put yourself in a position to receive God's direction for your life. Proverbs 3:5 - 6, tells us to *"Trust in the Lord with all thine heart; and lean not unto thine own understanding. In all thy ways acknowledge him, and He shall direct thy paths."*

Obedience to God requires that you are always willing to say as Jesus did in Luke 22:44, *"Father, if you are willing, take this cup from me; yet not my will, but yours be done."* Obedience to God will keep you calm amid difficulty and will bring you victory in the face of defeat. If you are obedient to God and His Word - no matter what you may see, think, or feel - you will be able to hear the still, small voice of the Holy Spirit says, *"Whether you turn to the right or to the left, your ears will hear a voice behind you, saying, "This is the way; walk in it."* (Isaiah 30:21).

Each of us must ask ourselves one important question when we face a crossroads in life: Will the path we choose be a path that will fulfill God's plan for our lives? Or will it simply be a path that follows our reasoning for what we want out of life?

Our choices are not always right but God's are. In Jeremiah 29:11, *"God says I know the plans I have for you, plans to prosper you and not to harm you, a plan to give you hope and a future."* I'm so glad that He has a plan for us – and it is always the right plan.

So, I have to ask, "Have you come to a "Cross" road in your life? Have you decided to decide to take up your cross and follow Jesus? Or have you decided to follow the flesh, the world, and Satan? Know that to NOT decide is a decision. So which path will you choose? God is saying – you're at a crossroads. Make a decision. Decide which road you're going to choose because Eternity hangs on the choice you make.

In the Sermon on the Mount, Jesus echoes Jeremiah's words. *"Enter through the narrow gate. For wide is the gate and broad is the road that leads to destruction, and many enter through it. But small is the gate and narrow the road that leads to life, and only a few find it."* (Matthew 7:13-14)

I want to encourage you to choose the narrow road. Don't assume that just because something is hard, it is not God's will. Jesus came to a Cross Road at the end of His life on earth. I call it a Cross Road, not because he was forced to make a choice, but because He willingly made a choice. It wasn't a choice to go to the left or the right. It was a choice to go all the way to Calvary. It was a choice to give His life for you and me.

~

Each of us must ask ourselves one important question when we face a crossroads in life: Will the path we choose be a path that will fulfill God's plan for our lives? Or will it simply be a path that follows our reasoning for what we want out of life? Know that our choices are not always right but God's choices are.

REFLECTION QUESTIONS:

1. Reflect on a recent "crossroad" situation in your life, how did you choose the path to take? In hindsight, what was the result of your choice? Did it bring glory to God?
2. Sometimes our reflection on the past causes us to have regrets about our past decisions. If that is the case for you, just remember that God works all things together for the good of those who love Him and the called according to His purpose.

CHAPTER 2

"YOU DON'T HAVE TO LOOK LIKE WHAT YOU'VE BEEN THROUGH"

On the morning of May 22, 1829, a slave ship called the Feloz was stopped on the open seas by a British Navy warship. This slave ship had taken in 562 individuals from the coast of Africa, 336 males and 226 females, and was headed for North America.

These Africans were chained below deck in a space so low that they couldn't stand but were forced to sit between each other's legs; and so close together that there was no possibility of lying down, standing up, or in any way, changing positions.

The Navy officer who had boarded this ship and was writing the report of his findings on the ship was astounded at how such a large number of human beings could exist in such conditions; packed and wedged together as tight as could be crammed, deep in the bowels of the ship where the men had an average space of 23 square inches and for the women only 13 inches. Not surprisingly, after 17 days at sea 55 individuals had died.

Those crammed conditions, combined with no toilet facilities and temperatures between 90 and 100 degrees produced an odor so offensive that it was almost impossible to enter where these Africans were chained. But the British officer and sailors did. After unshackling the adults and leading them to the top deck of the boat, they discovered in the nicks and crannies below deck, many children in a daze, who seemed indifferent to life or death.

The men, women, and children, now standing on the upper deck, out of the bowels of their nightmarish living quarters, saw air, water, and light as luxuries and shouted for joy with their weak voices. Upon reaching shore, the Navy Officer writing this report was informed by his friends who had visited many other slave ships that the conditions on the ship he captured were one of the best they had seen.

As we reflect on the lives of those 500 and the lives of millions of others who suffered and died in America through enslavement, then segregation, and continued bias, African Americans have proven time and time again that "You don't have to look like what you've been through."

Consider this passage of scripture from Job 28:1-13 and 28, *"There is a mine for silver and a place where gold is refined. Iron is taken from the earth, and copper is smelted from ore. Mortals put an end to the darkness; they search out the farthest recesses for ore in the blackest darkness. Far from human dwellings, they cut a shaft, in places untouched by human feet; far from other people they dangle and sway.*

"The earth, from which food comes, is transformed below by fire; lapis lazuli comes from its rocks, and its dust contains nuggets of gold. No bird of prey knows that hidden path, no falcon's eye has seen it. Proud beasts do not set foot on it, and no lion prowls there. People assault the flinty rock with their hands and lay bare the roots of the mountains. They tunnel through the rock; their eyes see all its treasures. They search the sources of the rivers and bring hidden things to light. But where can wisdom be found? Where does understanding dwell? No mortal comprehends its worth; it cannot be found in the land of the living." Verse 28 – *"And he said to the human race "The fear of the Lord—that is wisdom and to shun evil is understanding."*

Job went through heartache, hardships, and pain during his life. He was as low as you could go and compared his afflictions to hitting rock bottom. It was as if he had a target on his back and Satan kept hitting the bull's eye with the worst of the worst. Job lost everything he had - his children, his wealth, and even his health. And now he is making a connection between the creation of precious items and human hardship, suffering, and pain. He references silver and gold which we know is beautiful and valuable but it didn't always look that way. He references precious jewels such as diamonds that shine as bright as the sunshine but they didn't always look that way. They started in harsh conditions, below the earth, and didn't look very pretty.

Likewise, it's of value to reflect on the perseverance and faith of African Americans, who are an example that despite struggles, sorrows, heartaches, and pains, you don't have to look like, what you've been through.

But it's hard not to. When we are at our lowest point Satan will tell us that we ought to just give up and give in. That you don't need a relationship with God. And that drugs, alcohol, or something else that we put ahead of God, is the better solution.

But let me remind you that Satan is a liar because when we are at our lowest state, God will bring us out.

- Job thought he had lost it all – but God brought him out;
- Moses was a murderer hiding out in the desert but God made him the leader of God's people;
- Joseph was sold by his brothers and thrown in a pit and later in prison but God allowed him to save God's people;
- Elijah ran from Jezebel and was so depressed that he asked God to take his life – but God allowed a double portion of his anointing to be passed on to Elisha;
- Paul was knocked off his donkey on the Road to Damascus but God used him to write more than half of the New Testament; and
- Jesus was crucified and buried in a borrowed tomb but God raised Him from the grave.

Brothers and sisters God didn't bring you this far to leave you! *"Weeping endures for a night but joy comes in the morning."* (Psalm 30:5b) You don't have to look like what you've been through!

Someone may be saying "I've been through a lot; I've been beaten down; I've been abandoned by my friends and my family; I've had one setback after another; when I think it can't get any worse, it does. How do I NOT look like what I'm going through?"

Well, Job tells us that we can search with our eyes for treasures, for the hidden things but we won't find what we need. In verse 13 he tells us that no mortal can comprehend it because it's not found in the land of the living. But if you read verse 28, he says that the answer is wisdom. Godly wisdom tells us that when we are at our lowest state, it is there that God will work a miracle in our lives.

Godly wisdom from history tells us that despite years of slavery, despite being viewed as less than human, despite having no voting rights, despite having to attend second-class schools, despite having to sit in the back of the bus, despite seeing brothers, fathers, sisters, mothers hanging from trees, that at the appointed time God reminded us and all other oppressed people that He has a plan for us, a plan that includes a hope and a future. And you don't have to look like what you've gone through.

Godly wisdom tells us that we need to walk by faith and not by sight. That's why it was at the lowest state of their lives that songwriters wrote songs including . . .

- Nobody knows the trouble I've seen;
- Soon I will be done with the troubles of the world;
- Guide me Oh thou great Jehovah, pilgrim through this barren land; bread of heaven, bread of heaven, feed me til I want no more;
- Because He lives, I can face tomorrow, because He lives, all fear is gone;
- Father, I stretch my hand to thee, no other help I know;
- Pass me not O gentle Savior;
- I love the Lord, He heard my cry and pitied every groan;
- Can't nobody do me like Jesus;
- Jesus is on the mainline, call Him up and tell Him what you want;
- Jesus is a rock in a weary land; and
- Your grace and mercy brought me through, I'm living this moment because of you . . . I want to thank you and praise you too. Your grace and mercy brought me through.

I am reminded of the Mel Gibson movie of 2004 entitled "The Passion of Christ." It is one of the most realistic depictions of the horrendous, brutal crucifixion of Jesus Christ. Those final scenes were filled with images of Jesus . . . dirty, beaten and bloody. Bleeding from the crown of thorns pressed down on his head; bleeding from having the flesh ripped from his back with a whip that had metal in its tips; covered with dirt and sweat from carrying a 100-pound cross for almost half a mile. Then bleeding from the nails pounded through his hands and feet; later bleeding from the wound in his side.

In your imagination, can't you see his broken, bloody body pulled down from that old rugged cross, and placed in a borrowed tomb? Can you see Him? Hadn't He been through a lot? But you don't have to look like what you've gone through. Early on a Sunday morning, Jesus got up in all His glory. He didn't look like what He'd gone through and neither do you.

The bible tells us that if anyone is in Christ, he is a new creation; old things have passed away; behold, all things have become new; (2 Corinthians 5:17) and you won't look like what you've gone through. God said through Isaiah *"Do not remember the former things, Nor consider the things of old. Behold, I will do a new thing* (Isaiah 43:18-19). *You don't have to look like what you've gone through.*

Jeremiah said *"Because of the Lord's great love, we are not consumed, for his compassions never fail. They are new every morning* (Lamentations 3:22-23). *You don't have to look like what you've gone through.*

Paul said *"Do not lose heart. Though outwardly we are wasting away, yet inwardly we are being renewed day by day* (2 Corinthians 4:16-18). *You don't have to look like what you've gone through.*

Someone may have been told by the doctor that nothing can be done for their health condition. A family member may have said that you were no good. Or you were told that you'd never amount to anything. But look at you now! *You don't look like what you went through.*

~

REFLECTION QUESTIONS:

1. What positive changes in your life have you experienced over the past 5, 10, 20 years? What are the significant differences between "then and now?"
2. Consider a low point in your life, and reflect on your recovery journey. How did it occur? Who was influential in your changes?

CHAPTER 3

THE CHALLENGE OF LOVING LIKE THE LORD

Gary Inrig in his book, "True North, Discovering God's Way in a Changing World" quotes Tom Anderson who made a vow to himself as he drove with his family to spend two weeks at a vacation cottage. For two weeks he would try to be a loving husband and father. He decided after listening to a tape on his car's tape player. The speaker said, "Love is an act of the will. A person can choose to love." Tom admitted that he had been a selfish husband so he committed for two weeks to make changes.

Right from the moment they arrived at the vacation cottage, Tom kissed his wife Evelyn at the door and said, "That new yellow sweater looks great on you." "Oh, Tom, you noticed," she said, surprised and pleased; and maybe a little shocked.

After the long drive, Tom wanted to sit and read. Evelyn suggested a walk on the beach. He started to refuse, but then he thought, Evelyn's been alone with the kids at home and now she wants to be alone with me. He agreed and walked with his wife on the beach while their children flew their kites.

For two weeks Tom did not call the Wall Street investment firm where was a director. He did visit the Shell Museum, though he didn't like museums. His wife seemed so relaxed and happy he decided to keep remembering to choose love after they got home from vacation.

On the last night of their vacation, his wife stared at him with the saddest expression. Tom asked her, "What's the matter? "Tom," she said, in a voice filled with distress, "do you know something I don't?"

"What do you mean?" "Well, …that checkup I had several weeks ago…our doctor…did he tell you something about me? Tom, you've been so good to me…am I dying?

It took a moment for it all to sink in. Then Tom burst out laughing. "No, honey," he said, wrapping her in his arms, "you're not dying; I'm just starting to live."

In Matthew 22:35 – 40, Jesus is answering questions asked of Him by the Sadducees and the Pharisees. *"One of them, an expert in the law, tested him with this question: "Teacher, which is the greatest commandment in the Law?" Jesus replied: "'Love the Lord **your** God with all your heart and with all your soul and with all your mind.' This is the first and greatest commandment. And the second is like it: 'Love your neighbor as yourself.' All the Law and the Prophets hang on these two commandments."*

Sadducees were a Jewish sect that denied the resurrection of the dead, the existence of spirits, and emphasized the authority of the written Law alone. Pharisees believed in resurrection and in following legal traditions including paying taxes. Jesus in response to another question advised that Jews should *"Give to Caesar what belongs to Caesar."* (Mark 12:17)

However, in this instance, Jesus responds to the Sadducees' question, "Which is the greatest commandment in the Law?" by articulating that the key concept is "Relationships." We are to have a **vertical** relationship with the Divine – "Love the Lord **your** God with all your heart and with all your soul and with all your mind' and have **horizontal** relationships with our fellowman – "Love your neighbor as yourself."

But what are the fundamental characteristics of those relationships? Well, if we look closely at Jesus' response, we see that those two dimensions of the Great Commandment begin with one word – LOVE. "**Love** your God" and "**Love** your neighbor."

In **1 Corinthians 13:1 – 13, Paul says** *"If I speak in the tongues of men or of angels, but do not have love, I am only a resounding gong or a clanging cymbal. If I have the gift of prophecy and can fathom all mysteries and all knowledge, and if I have a faith that can move mountains, but do not have love, I am nothing. If I give all I possess to the poor and give over my body to hardship that I may boast, but do not have love, I gain nothing. Love is patient,* *love is kind. It does not envy, it does not boast, it is not proud. It does not dishonor others, it is not self-seeking, it is not easily angered, it keeps no record of wrongs. Love does not delight in evil but rejoices with the truth. It always protects, always trusts, always hopes, always perseveres. Love never fails. But where there are prophecies, they will cease; where there are tongues, they will be stilled; where there is knowledge, it will pass away.*

And then in the 13th verse he says, *"And now these three remain - faith, hope and love. But the greatest of these is love."*

So Jesus tells us that the greatest commandment is to love the Lord with body, mind and soul **and** neighbor as yourself. Paul tells us in 1st Corinthians 13 that no matter how gifted we are – no matter how successful in ministry – no matter how religious we might be – there is one overarching principle that should guide everything we do, and that is to love like Jesus.

If we don't have love as the foundation for all of our relationships, then everything else is for naught. Just as a seed will not grow without soil, so the fruit of the Spirit will not grow except in the context of love.

Now love is an interesting word. We use it in so many different ways: I love my wife; I love fried catfish; I love pound cake; and I love the Golden State Warriors. And I'm sure you've heard that there are different types of love ...

- **Storge** – love between family members;
- **Eros** – physical love or sexual desire
- **Phileo** - brotherly love or friendship. The city of Philadelphia gets its name from this word.

But neither of these types of love can make a lasting difference in this sin-sick world because they last only as long as you say you love me; or as long as things are right between us; or as long as I'm getting what I want out of the relationship.

Jesus talked about another type of love in John 15:12-13. He said, *"My command is this: Love each other as I have loved you. Greater love has no one than this, that he lay down his life for his friends."* We call this Agape or selfless love – the love of God towards us. It is the type of love that defines the very character of God.

In that love chapter found in 1 Corinthians chapter 13, Paul tells us that to love like Jesus, you must understand five things:

First, conspicuous spirituality without love means absolutely nothing. Paul said, *"If I speak in the tongues of men or of angels, but do not have love, I am only a resounding gong or a clanging cymbal."* (1 Corinthians 13:1) In other words, even if you can teach or preach the Word of God but don't have love, you've missed the boat. Do you know of someone who can sing a hymn or pray a prayer that brings others to tears? Or preach to make the congregation dance and shout, Hallelujah? Paul is telling us that all of these talents put together mean absolutely nothing if you're not willing to love like Jesus.

Second, limitless knowledge without love means absolutely nothing. In 1 Corinthians 13:2 Paul says, *"And though I have the gift of prophecy, and understand all mysteries, and all knowledge; I am nothing."* Knowledge is extremely important but it is not the only answer for the problems of society today. Knowing the Bible backwards and forwards, being able to cite chapter and verse is good but you can't please God without loving everyone! Education of the head won't change the condition of the heart. I know a few smart but hard-hearted people.

Then in the 2nd part of 1 Corinthians 13:2, Paul tells us that extreme faith without love means absolutely nothing. He says, *"If I have a faith that can move mountains, but do not have love, I am nothing."* All Christians have faith; you can't please God without it. (Hebrews 11:6) But some Christians have extreme faith - mountain-moving faith; faith to trust God for great things. But even the most extreme faith, equals absolutely nothing if there is little love in your heart!

And in 1 Corinthians 13:3, Paul tells us that awesome generosity without love means absolutely nothing. He writes, *"If I give all I possess to the poor, but do not have love, I gain nothing."* People give to the poor, to their favorite charities, and even to the church for all kinds of reasons: sometimes out of guilt; sometimes to impress other people. Some men give to their wives when they're in the doghouse; some parents give elaborate Christmas gifts to their children to show their love for their children.

But self-sacrifice doesn't always come from a place of true love. And Paul says that the mere act of giving, even generously, while it might help those who receive, is worthless to the giver if the reason behind it is not love.

Finally, Paul says even making the ultimate sacrifice without love means absolutely nothing. He continues in 1 Corinthians 13:3, *"And even if I give over my body to hardship that I may boast, but do not have love, I gain nothing."* Without love in one's heart, even a willingness to sacrifice physically including a willingness to give up one's life, might impress people, and get you on the news, but it is not going to please God if your motive is not love!

According to Paul, without love, everything you do in your relationships and even in the church means nothing; you're nothing but a fake and a phony. Then in 1 Corinthians 13:13, Paul has a final word to say about love – *"And now these three remain: faith, hope and love. But the greatest of these is love."*

So, no matter what else you might get right or have going for yourself if you don't love like Jesus, everything else amounts to absolutely nothing. Our challenge is to build our relationships on a foundation of love that never fails. Jesus said in John 13:35, *"By this, all men will know that you are My disciples, if you have love for one another."* Jesus wasn't just talking about having nice thoughts toward others, which no one else can see. He was talking about love that can be seen. Because love stems from the heart, but love has to be seen in outward actions.

Well, if we return to Mark 12:30-31, we are told to "Love your God" and to "Love your neighbor." The word "YOUR" makes this commandment, personal. When we consider the types of relationships that we can have, I need to tell you that you can have a relationship with someone and it is not necessarily a personal one.

Your doctor or lawyer or school teacher can spend time with you and can do things for you but we would all agree that those relationships are not personal. Does your doctor call you up just to say hello? Does your lawyer invite you to their home for dinner?

If we consider the relationships that Jesus had with His disciples, some were more personal than others. In Luke 10:1, we read that Jesus *"appointed seventy-two and sent them two by two ahead of Him to every town and place where He was about to go."* In Mark 3:14, we read that *"He appointed twelve that they might be with him and that he might send them out to preach."*

In various scripture passages, we read that Jesus took Peter, James, and John to the Mount of Transfiguration; into the home where he raised the little girl from the dead and into the Garden of Gethsemane the night that He was betrayed. And then there was John who was called four times as "the disciple whom Jesus loved." So, if we are going to love like Jesus, our relationships should be personal.

In the 10th chapter of Luke, Jesus continues His conversation with the Sadducees and Pharisees who ask a follow-up question in verse 29, "Who is my neighbor?" To answer his question, in verses 30 -37, Jesus shares a parable about a man who was beaten and tossed on the side of the road by robbers. Three people pass this man on the road from Jericho to Jerusalem. The first man is a priest (pastor), the second man is a Levite (deacon) and the third is not even a member of the church, he's a Samaritan.

The first two men passed by the beaten man without helping him, while the third stopped to help the man. The Samaritan takes him into town, pays for his care, and even promises to pay for any additional expenses.

In verse 36 *Jesus asks, "Which of these three do you think was a neighbor to the man who fell into the hands of robbers?" 37 The expert in the law replied, "The one who had mercy on him." Jesus told him, "Go and do likewise."*

This parable clearly identifies our neighbor as anyone, not just those who live next door or near you. And clearly the Samaritan demonstrated love for the injured man but we don't know whether the Samaritan ever developed a personal relationship with the man. God not only wants us to show love, but He wants our love to bear the fruit of a personal relationship with Him and with one another.

We can have a personal relationship with God because it was, He Who so loved the world, that he gave his only Son, that whoever believes in him should not perish but have eternal life. That's the kind of love, God expects of us.

And then look at Jesus' love - Who *"while we were still sinners, Christ died for us. Greater love has no one than this: to lay down one's life for one's friends."* (Romans 5:8) That's the kind of love, God expects of us.

Whether your spouse loves you, whether your mom and daddy love you, whether your children love you, whether your friends love you, Christ loves you and you can count on Him! Whatever is troubling you, the good news is that because of God's love, you can have a personal relationship with Jesus and because of that relationship, help is on the way!!!

The songwriter said, "I was sinking deep in sin, far from the peaceful shore, very deeply stained within, sinking to rise no more; but the Master of the sea heard my despairing cry, from the waters lifted me now safe am I. Love lifted me. When nothing else could help love lifted me."

So, when trouble is occurring in your life, don't look to Capitol Hill, look to Calvary's Hill and call on Jesus! The author and finisher of our faith. The One who can do everything but fail. The One who said, *"Father prepare me a body and I'll go."* (Hebrews 10:5)

You were created to know God in a personal way—to have a relationship with Him, through His Son, Jesus Christ. The One who said *"As the Father loved Me, I also have loved you; abide in My love. If you keep My commandments, you will abide in My love, just as I have kept My Father's commandments and abide in His love. "These things I have spoken to you, that My joy may remain in you, and that your joy may be full. This is My commandment, that you love one another as I have loved you. Greater love has no one than this, than to lay down one's life for his friends."* (John 15:9-13)

Loving like Jesus is the best way to live. When we love like Him, we can shed layers of selfishness, resentment, anxiety, pettiness, and entitlement. Remember Jesus said, *"A new commandment I give to you, that you love one another: just as I have loved you, you also are to love one another."* (John 13:34) That's the challenge for each of us today.

≈

God tells us to show kindness to others because that is part of His wonderful character. And if He dwells inside of us, then what we do including how we love, should be reflected in whose we are. That's the kind of loving God we need to show this world. It's not enough for us to say we love others; we must show it. The Son of God, Jesus the Christ, didn't just tell us that He loves us, He showed it. Romans 5:8 says, *"While we were still sinners, Christ died for us."*

REFLECTION QUESTIONS FOR YOU:

1. What is something that you do that shows your love for God and your neighbor?
2. Is there something that you can do to show more love for God and your neighbor?

CHAPTER 4

THE NECESSITY & BLESSING OF FORGIVENESS

"Today upon a bus, I saw a lovely maid with golden hair; I envied her -- she seemed so gay, and how, I wished I were so fair; When suddenly she rose to leave, I saw her hobble down the aisle; she had one foot and wore a crutch, but as she passed, a smile. Oh God, forgive me when I whine, I have two feet -- the world is mine.

"And when I stopped to buy some sweets, the lad who served me had such charm; he seemed to radiate good cheer, and his manner was so kind and warm; I said, "It's nice to deal with you, such courtesy I seldom find"; he turned and said, "Oh, thank you sir." And then I saw that he was blind. Oh, God, forgive me when I whine, I have two eyes, and the world is mine.

"Then, while walking down the street, I saw a child with eyes of blue; he stood and watched the others play, it seemed he knew not what to do; I stopped a moment, then I said, "Why don't you join the others, dear?" He looked ahead without a word, and then I knew he could not hear. Oh God, forgive me when I whine, I have two ears, and the world is mine.

"With feet to take me where I'd go; with eyes to see the sunsets glow, with ears to hear what I would know. I am blessed indeed. The world is mine; oh, God, forgive me when I whine." (Poem by Red Foley)

Christians often face the challenge of forgiveness - forgiving others and even forgiving themselves. In the 18th chapter of Matthew, we see Jesus teaching on several major themes. In verses 1 – 5, He answers the disciples' question about status, and greatness with the life lesson that we need to be as humble as a child. In verses 6 – 9, Jesus warns about the danger of leading others into sin. In verses 10 – 14, He uses the analogy of sheep to emphasize the necessity of seeking the lost (leave the 99 to find the 1). In verses 15 – 20, we are given guidance on how to deal with another Christian who is engaged in sin (1 on 1; 1 or 2 witnesses; then before the church).

And then beginning with verse 21, Jesus tells a parable of an unforgiving servant to challenge us to Forgive.

> *"Then Peter came to Jesus and asked, "Lord, how many times shall I forgive my brother or sister who sins against me? Up to seven times?" Jesus answered, "I tell you, not seven times, but seventy-seven times. "Therefore, the kingdom of heaven is like a king who wanted to settle accounts with his servants.*

> *As he began the settlement, a man who owed him ten thousand bags of gold was brought to him. Since he was not able to pay, the master ordered that he and his wife and his children and all that he had to be sold to repay the debt. "At this, the servant fell on his knees before him. 'Be patient with me,' he begged, 'and I will pay back everything.' The servant's master took pity on him, canceled the debt, and let him go.*

> *"But when that servant went out, he found one of his fellow servants who owed him a hundred silver coins. He grabbed him and began to choke him. 'Pay back what you owe me!' he demanded. "His fellow servant fell to his knees and begged him, 'Be patient with me, and I will pay it back.' "But he refused. Instead, he went off and had the man thrown into prison until he could pay the debt.*

> *When the other servants saw what had happened, they were outraged and went and told their master everything that had happened. "Then the master called the servant in. 'You wicked servant,' he said, 'I canceled all that debt of yours*

*because you begged me to. Shouldn't you have had mercy on
your fellow servant just as I had on you?' In anger, his master
handed him over to the jailers to be tortured, until he should
pay back all he owed.*

*"This is how my heavenly Father will treat each of you unless
you forgive your brother or sister from your heart."*

When someone has hurt us, we sometimes keep stewing about it over
and over again. We may put it out of our minds for a while, but whenever
we see that person or think about the hurtful thing they did to us, how
unfair it was, how terrible they are for having done that to us; we may even
wonder how we can give them some payback.

And then sometimes, we think about our own mistakes, what we did
wrong, and how we should have avoided the hurt done to a family member,
friend, or even a stranger. Unfortunately, we not only have difficulty
forgiving others but sometimes have difficulty forgiving ourselves.

Well, there is good news available for both of these situations. God has
a solution that if applied, will restore what the flesh corrodes. It's called,
Forgiveness.

Forgiveness is a foundational principle to Christian living because, at
one time or another, we will all struggle with issues of anger, resentment,
and bitterness as a result of mistreatment or mistakes by others towards us.
But thanks be to God, we've been given four keys to receive the blessing
of forgiveness.

First, forgiveness is a command, not a suggestion. When Jesus
taught His disciples how to pray in Matthew 6:14-15, He said that they
should ask God to forgive us our trespasses **as we forgive those who
trespass** against us. This was such a key spiritual principle and a directive
from God that Jesus gave this immediate warning, *"if you do not forgive
men their trespasses, neither will your Father forgive your trespasses."*

Paul puts it this way in Colossians 3:12-13 - *"as the elect of God, holy and
beloved, put on tender mercies, kindness, humility, meekness, longsuffering;
bearing with one another, and **forgiving one another** if anyone has a
complaint against another; even as Christ forgave you, so you also **must do**.*

In addition to forgiving others, we must be willing to forgive ourselves for the wrong we've done to others. Psalms 103:10-11 tells us that God *"does not treat us as our sins deserve or repay us according to our iniquities. For as high as the heavens are above the earth, so great is his love for those who fear him."*

Therefore, all we have to do is repent of our past wrong choices and God wipes the slate clean. *"If we confess our sins, He is faithful and just to forgive us our sins and to cleanse us from all unrighteousness."* (1 John 1:9) In other words, just tell God where you went wrong, that you are sorry, and He will take care of everything else and wash it away—transforming you into a new creature. And if God is willing to forgive us, we should be willing to do so as well.

Second, our Forgiveness of others should have no limit. In Matthew 18:21-22, *Peter came to Jesus and said, "Lord, how often shall my brother sin against me, and I forgive him? Up to seven times?" Jesus said to him, "I do not say to you, up to seven times, but up to seventy times seven.*

Jesus didn't mean to forgive 490 times and stop. He used simple mathematics to say that our forgiveness of others should be **limitless.** If you're keeping score, then you're missing the point. Let me ask, "How many times do you want to be forgiven by the Lord?" Do you want Him to have a maximum number and once He reaches His maximum, that's it? We've all hit that number and then some. Amen?

Now, let's be clear - forgiveness does not mean that when someone hurts you it doesn't matter. It does matter. We're hurt – physically, and emotionally. But it's not up to us to get payback or that pound of flesh. Romans 12:19 tells us that we are "not to take revenge, but leave room for God's wrath, for it is written (in Deuteronomy 32:35): *"It is mine to avenge; I will repay," says the Lord.*

At the same time, the Lord expects us to be smart about how we live our lives. In Matthew 10:16, *Jesus said, "Behold, I send you out as sheep in the midst of wolves. Therefore be wise as serpents and harmless as doves."* In other words, if you get bitten by a snake that lives in a hole, don't continue to put your hand in the same hole. So, while being smart, we need to learn to forgive as God forgives. His Forgiveness is limitless, and so should ours.

Third, not forgiving others is costly. In this 18th chapter of Matthew, we see that the servant owed a debt of 10,000 talents to his master. To put this into perspective, 10,000 talents would be worth over 7 billion dollars today. Since a good day's wage was 1 denarii or the equivalent of 62 cents, the bottom line is that the man could never pay the debt owed –even if he worked every day from the foundation of the world until the end of time. Yet he was forgiven.

But the servant that owed more than he could pay was forgiven, yet he refused to forgive another. And because of his unwillingness to forgive we see in the Matthew 18:34 that "**He was delivered to the torturers.**"

When we refuse to forgive others, we are telling God that we don't want Him to forgive us of our sins. In Matthew 18:35 *Jesus says, "My heavenly Father also will do to you, if each of you, from his heart, does not forgive his brother his trespasses."*

It has been said that unforgiveness is like drinking a cup of poison, hoping it hurts the other person. The truth is that when we cling to anger, even though it may have been years since we were wronged, we hurt ourselves, not the person who wronged us. The bitterness that you hold inside, will eat you up physically and can lead to high blood pressure, headaches, and heart attacks.

We throw a pity party that only we can attend. We can't enjoy life and those around us can't either. We're so focused on clinging to old hurts from the past that we miss out on the blessings of today. Consequently, it is difficult to form a new relationship or have a healthy relationship until you heal the hurt and upsets of your past.

And let's not forget that our bitterness towards others or personal guilt does nothing but play into Satan's hands who seeks to kill, steal, and destroy. You can't praise God, you can't help someone in need, and you can't have a beautiful relationship if you are filled with bitterness or guilt.

On the other hand, forgiveness is accepting the fact that you can't change the past. Forgiveness is also knowing that whoever hurt you in the past, no longer has power over you. When you forgive, you're set free. It is never too late to forgive or be forgiven.

Finally, in addition to unforgiveness being costly, Forgiveness is an intentional, spiritual act. Unfortunately, some people will say, "I haven't heard the Lord tell me to forgive them yet." Yes, forgiveness is difficult sometimes. Forgiveness is also not just a feeling or something you think about. It is a conscious, voluntary decision led by the Holy

Spirit - not by the flesh. Forgiveness is a decision we make to do what is right before God, and then we do it.

Paul tells us that we must command our minds to be subject to the Holy Spirit. In Romans 12:14-18, he says, *"Bless those who persecute you; bless and do not curse. Rejoice with those who rejoice, and weep with those who weep. Be of the same mind toward one another. Do not set your mind on high things, but associate with the humble. Do not be wise in your own opinion.* **Repay no one evil for evil.** *Have regard for good things in the sight of all men. If it is possible, as much as depends on you,* **live peaceably with all men."** **Forgiveness is voluntary, it is intentional and it is spiritual.**

The gospel record tells us about one of the greatest voluntary acts of forgiveness. Jesus Christ has been betrayed, arrested, tried, denied, mocked, scorned, and tortured. With an old rugged cross on His bloodied back, he has been marched up to Calvary, nailed to a Cross, and now at 9:00 a.m. hangs between heaven and earth with a thief on his left and a thief on his right.

The gospel record tells us that as He hangs in agony, He opens not His mouth to curse His abusers or His haters. He opens not His mouth to call 10,000 angels to escort Him from the horrors of the cross to His heavenly throne.

With blood and water flowing from His pierced side, He prayed for mankind's greatest need - *"Father, forgive them for they know not what they do."* (Luke 23:34)

With a sinner mocking him on his left and enemies all around Him, He did not pray for their destruction but prayed for our salvation - "Father, forgive them for they know not what they do."

When the sun refused to shine and the Father turned His back on Him, He did not pray for His deliverance, but prayed, "Father, forgive them for they know not what they do."

When the earth rocked and reeled and the dead climbed out of their graves, imagine Jesus saying, Father. . .

- Forgive my enemies, Caiaphas, the Sanhedrin; Pilate and Herod who judged and condemned me;
- Forgive the fickle crowd, who praised me on Sunday and rejected me on Wednesday;

- Forgive my Apostles who walked with me for over 3 years but have now deserted me;
- Forgive Peter who on one day declared that I am the Christ but less than 12 hours later denied Me three times,
- Forgive the soldiers who scourged me, mocked me, tortured me, and nailed me to this cross.

That's what we might hear in our imagination but the gospel record gives only these words, "Father, forgive them, for they know not what they do."

At the height of his physical suffering, Jesus's Divine love prevails. And now hanging on an old rugged cross, Jesus prays, that the Father give them the one thing every sinner needs – Forgiveness.

If you are feeling shame or regret, if the Lord's forgiveness seems out of reach, know that God is both just and merciful. The Psalmist said *"As far as the east is from the west, so far has He removed our transgressions from us."* (Psalm 103:12). And God wants to forgive you, and all you have to do is ask.

REFLECTION QUESTIONS:

1. What slight, misdeed or mistreatment by another are you holding on to? Is it time to let it go?
2. What slight, misdeed or mistreatment to another do you regret and have not forgiven yourself of having committed?

CHAPTER 5

FAITH – GOD'S SOLUTION FOR OUR DOUBTS & UNBELIEF

"Desperate to find a home, an orphan girl in India asked a missionary teacher from a nearby village for help. The missionary had no money or room for the girl but promised she'd pray and ask God for his help. She told the girl to do the same.

That evening, the teacher received a letter from an American friend, containing enough money to provide for the orphan girl. She summoned a messenger the following morning and asked him to go to the neighboring village--a day's walk from her home--to find the girl.

To the teacher's surprise, the messenger returned with the girl in half the expected time. When asked how she traveled so quickly, the girl reminded the teacher, "We both prayed to God for help...I thought I might as well start walking." (Author Unknown)

Faith is active. Thinking and praying are necessary elements, but the true test of our faith is when like the little girl, we start walking.

Matthew, Mark, and Luke record that about a week after Jesus told His disciples that He would suffer, be killed, and be raised to life, He took Peter, James, and John up a mountain to pray. While praying, His appearance was changed into a glorified form, and His clothing became dazzling white. Moses and Elijah appeared and talked with Jesus about the death that He would soon suffer. Then a cloud wrapped around them and a voice said, "This is My Son, whom I have chosen, whom I love; listen to Him!" (Matthew 17:5)

Then the cloud lifted, Moses and Elijah disappeared, and Jesus was alone with His disciples who were shocked and afraid from what they had just seen. Jesus warned them not to tell anyone what they had seen until after His resurrection.

Following this event, called the "Transfiguration", in the 17th chapter of Matthew, in verses 14 – 21, we read of a father with a child who has been sick from birth.

> *"And when they had come to the multitude, a man came to Him, kneeling to Him and saying, "Lord, have mercy on my son, for he is [c]an epileptic and suffers severely; for he often falls into the fire and often into the water. 16 So I brought him to Your disciples, but they could not cure him."*
>
> *Then Jesus answered and said, "O faithless and perverse generation, how long shall I be with you? How long shall I bear with you? Bring him here to Me." And Jesus rebuked the demon, and it came out of him, and the child was cured from that very hour.*
>
> *Then the disciples came to Jesus privately and said, "Why could we not cast it out?" So Jesus said to them, "Because of your unbelief; for assuredly, I say to you, if you have faith as a mustard seed, you will say to this mountain, 'Move from here to there,' and it will move; and nothing will be impossible for you. 21 However, this kind does not go out except by prayer and fasting."* (Matthew 17:14-21)

This is a father who has done what any loving father would do. He's made significant sacrifices and probably has been to every doctor and healer in town looking for a cure, but no help was found.

Matthew also tells us that this father had sought help from Jesus' disciples but the disciples weren't able to help the child either. In verse 17 Jesus referred to them as a "faithless and twisted generation." Mark records Jesus calling them *"an unbelieving generation."* (Mark 9:19)

There was another generation whose faith was challenged many years before. The Children of Israel had been freed from Egyptian captivity but Pharaoh changed his mind and was now in hot pursuit of them. The Israelites are on foot, with no weapons, carrying all of their earthly belongings.

While camped on the shore of the Red Sea which is 8 miles wide and 300 feet deep, the entire Egyptian army on chariots, horses, and on foot can be seen rushing to catch them. Some even complained to Moses, saying they should have remained in Egypt since there were graveyards there. They are in the midst of what some would call an impossible situation.

But God challenged them to remain faithful as they were trapped between pharaoh's army behind them and the Red Sea in front of them. And we know the rest of the story . . . God showed up and showed out. His people were delivered and their enemy was destroyed.

Well, many believers in Jesus Christ have had or will have a Red Sea experience. A situation that will cause our faith to falter, our trust to be tested, and our dependence on the Lord to be disturbed. A situation that to us, seems utterly impossible. A situation where we find ourselves hemmed in by circumstances, enemies, obstacles, and life's problems. A situation that discourages, disappoints, and depresses. A situation that may cause you to say to yourself, I'm at the Red Sea of my life, pharaoh is about to run me down – I might as well just give up because I can't go forward and I can't go backward.

Well in the case of the father's sick child, Jesus' disciples had run into a difficult situation. One that they were not able to handle. In Matthew 17:19 they ask Jesus, *"Why could we not cast it out?"*

Jesus' answer is wisdom for each of us. He said, *"Because you have so little faith."* (Matthew 17:20) In other words the problem was their unbelief. Then Jesus, as He does so many times, not only rebukes and tells His disciples that they had no faith, but He tells them how to fix the problem. In Matthew 17:21 Jesus says, *"This kind does not go out except by prayer and fasting."* What did Jesus mean?

First of all, "this kind" refers to a difficult situation. Difficult situations can't be handled by ordinary solutions. When you fast and pray, you have gotten serious about your desire to connect with the Lord and to walk in victory. And when we connect with God in such a deep way, He knows just how serious we are!

Fasting and prayer give us access to God's presence and power because we deny the physical to focus on the spiritual. So let me suggest that when standing at the edge of your Red Sea, fast and pray. Ask the Lord to grant you the strength to meet the challenges to your faith.

And the Lord will tell you don't worry because worry never solved a problem; worry never paid a debt; worry never alleviated a pain; worry never made an enemy your friend; and worry never turned a wrong into a right. Some would say that worry is the interest paid on a loan that you haven't even taken out yet.

Psalm 37:1 says, *"Do not fret because of evil men or be envious of those who do wrong…"* And Paul tells us in Philippians 4:6-7, *"Do not be anxious about anything, but in everything by prayer and supplication with thanksgiving, let your requests be made known to God. And the peace of God, which surpasses all understanding will guard your hearts and your minds in Christ Jesus."*

Instead of worrying or doubting, just *"Trust in the Lord with all your heart and lean not on your understanding; in all your ways acknowledge Him and He will direct your paths."* (Proverbs 3:5-6)

The Lord will also tell you to not be afraid. Fear is a close relative to worry because both worry and fear will paralyze you. Too many folks today are living in bondage to fear. The fear of death, fear of sickness, fear of failure, fear of poverty, fear of being alone, and even the fear of germs.

Fear is one of the greatest enemies of faith. Fear will turn love into hate. The rattlesnake strikes, the dog bites, and the cat scratches when they are afraid. The same is true of a person who is afraid. Back a person into a corner, make them afraid and there is no telling what they will do.

Fear will also cause us to turn to what the world offers to find peace - alcohol, drugs, or some otherworldly pleasure. But Isaiah 41:10 said, *"Fear not, for I am with you; do not be dismayed, for I am your God: I will strengthen you, I will uphold you with the right hand of my righteousness."*

David said, "Even though I walk through the darkest valley, I will fear no evil, for you are with me;" (Psalm 23:4). And Paul tells us in 2 Timothy 1:7, that *"God has not given us a spirit of fear, but of power and love and a sound mind.*

So, trust and remain faithful during your Red Sea situation. The father who sought help from Jesus didn't give up and he didn't give in. He pressed on, looking for a solution for his son's situation. Galatians 6:3 tells us that: *"We shall reap if we faint not."* We define fainting as being exhausted but from the original Greek language, to faint means to be utterly spiritless, to fail in heart, or to be discouraged. God told Moses and the Israelites when faced with their Red Sea situation to go forward – to trust God despite how difficult the situation looks.

Likewise, we must step out on faith. No matter how difficult the situation looks to you, be willing to embrace the uncertainty to see the unbelievable. Remember that -

- By faith, Noah survived a great flood;
- By faith, Abraham found a ram in the bush;
- By faith, the walls of Jericho crumbled into dust;
- By faith, David slew a giant with a boy's toy;
- By faith, Daniel made a hungry lion his pillow; and
- By faith, 3 Hebrew boys had a little talk with Jesus in a fiery furnace.

All we have to do is walk by faith, not by sight. Because looks can be deceiving! When we look at things through our eyes, we see doubt. But If we see things as God does, we see the victory.

So, we have to be willing to stay on the battlefield for our Lord. Isaiah said that those who wait on the Lord (that takes faith), will mount up with wings like eagles, will run and not be weary - will walk and not faint. (Isaiah 40:31)

When you trust God, know that He will fight your battle. He'll turn your night into day and give you peace in the middle of your storm. Jesus is able to do everything but fail. He healed the sick; made the cripple walk, the blind see and the deaf hear. He turned water into wine, cast out demons, and made the dead live again.

But that was not why He came. He came to give His life on Calvary. And as the songwriter says, "Because He lives, we can face tomorrow. Because He lives, all fear is gone. Because I know He holds the future. And life is worth the living just because He lives."

~

While God is not looking for perfect people (because there are none), He is looking for faithful people. 1 Corinthians 4:2 clearly states that *"it is required that those who have been given a trust must prove faithful."* And in Luke 17:5, *the apostles said to the Lord, "Increase our faith!"* So how do you increase or grow your faith? To grow in faith, we must develop at least two habits: The habit of Feeding on the Word of God and the habit of Communing with the Lord. A habit is when you do something so regularly, so repeatedly, that it becomes automatic. You don't have to think about doing the thing anymore.

If you only feed on the Word of God on Sunday, you won't have the strength to fight, the strength to remain encouraged, the strength to withstand the attacks of the devil, the temptations of the flesh, and the attractions of the world. Therefore, if you want to grow your faith, come to Sunday worship, have your personal study time, and come to midweek bible study, and have others that you can discuss the Word with. Then find a place to serve, a place to do, to exercise what we are instructed to do.

The second primary spiritual habit we need to develop is the habit of prayer. Jesus prayed often and taught His disciples to pray. Prayer has to become a habit.

REFLECTION QUESTIONS:

1. Examine your faith today, is it growing?
2. Are you on a regular diet of healthy spiritual food?
3. Do you have a regular time of private time with the Lord? If not set one and make it a habit.

CHAPTER 6

ADVERSITY: DOWN BUT NOT OUT

"Two hunters came across a bear so big that they dropped their rifles and ran for their lives. One man climbed a tree while the other hid in a nearby cave. The bear was in no hurry to eat, so he sat down between the tree and the cave to reflect upon his good fortune. Suddenly, and for no apparent reason, the hunter in the cave came running out, almost ran into the waiting bear, hesitated, and then ran back into the cave. The same thing happened a second time. When he ran out the third time, his buddy in the tree shouted out, "Have you lost your mind? Stay in the cave till he leaves!" His buddy said, "I can't, there's another bear in the cave."

Do you ever feel like the hunter in the cave? Every time you turn around there is another problem just waiting for you. And sure enough, life is filled with issues, trials, and struggles. The truth of the matter is that sometimes we can do everything right and life still goes wrong.

Well, some refer to life as a school – a school of hard knocks. Others say that adversity is the greatest university because the most long-lasting lessons in life happen through adversity. It has also been said that adversity introduces a person to themselves because you'll never know yourself until you've been tested by adversity.

Let me share a truth with you. Adversity is not a choice. If it were, we would say no thanks. But we live in a fallen world where there is sin and Satan. *Jesus Christ said, "I have told you these things, so that in me you may have peace. In this world you will have trouble. But take heart! I have overcome the world.""* (John 16:33) So, without a doubt, we will all experience adversity at one time or another but let me suggest that suffering is optional.

Let's take a look at adversity. An exploration through various dictionaries results in synonyms for adversity including misfortune, a troubling situation, or hardship. Charles Stanley defined it as a condition of suffering and hardship involving anguish, pressure, trials, heartaches, and disappointments. Have you experienced any of those things in life? Yes, Adversity is not optional but suffering is a choice because we can choose how to handle it. Well in this 4th chapter of 2 Corinthians verses 7-9, Paul addresses the issue of adversity.

> *"But we have this treasure in jars of clay to show that this all-surpassing power is from God and not from us. We are hard pressed on every side, but not crushed; perplexed, but not in despair; persecuted, but not abandoned; struck down, but not destroyed."*

> *And in verses 16-18: "Therefore, we do not lose heart. Though outwardly we are wasting away, yet inwardly we are being renewed day by day. 17 For our light and momentary troubles are achieving for us an eternal glory that far outweighs them all. 18 So we fix our eyes not on what is seen, but on what is unseen, since what is seen is temporary, but what is unseen is eternal."*

Paul is telling the church at Corinth and Christians today, that they are special. Why? In 2 Corinthians 4:7 verse, Paul tells us that *"we have this treasure in jars of clay to show that this all-surpassing power is from God and not from us."*

What is this treasure? – The gospel of Jesus Christ, the Power of the Holy Spirit, and the promises of God. What are the jars of clay? Figuratively speaking, that's you and I, in the flesh. Whose power is available to us but not our own? The power of God. If you are a believer, that makes you special.

In 2 Corinthians 4:8 & 9, Paul provides a contrast and comparison between the reality of adversity and the power of God. He writes,

- hard pressed on every side, but not crushed;
- perplexed, but not in despair;
- persecuted, but not abandoned;
- struck down, but not destroyed.

The first clause in each phrase speaks to what happens to us when adversity strikes – hard pressed, perplexed, persecuted, and struct down. The second clause, speaks to the power of God in us – not crushed, not in despair, not abandoned and not destroyed. That's why we're special.

The first two phrases describe how trouble can affect us on the inside – hard-pressed, perplexed. The second two clauses describe how trouble can come at us from the outside – persecuted, struck down.

Yes, this world is full of stresses - things that press up against us & pressure us. Paul makes it plain that whoever we are - we are never free from one trial or another put upon us by all sorts of persons – not just enemies but family, friends, and even children of God.

And not only are we stressed by people and situations in life but we are also persecuted by the enemy himself – the devil. If you are a born-again believer in Jesus Christ as Lord and Savior, then you are a spiritual being and you are living in the midst of a spiritual world. And in the midst of this spiritual world, we don't wrestle against flesh & blood but we wrestle against principalities & powers & strongholds of darkness & spiritual rulers in the heavenly realms. (Ephesians 6:12)

We wrestle against spiritual forces and they are real! We are under constant attack by Satan, who Peter said wanders about as a roaring lion seeking whom he may devour. (1 Peter 5:8) Satan intends to pull us away from our relationship with the Lord and by doing so, stop us from doing the Lord's work. Satan knows that when we are pressed and persecuted, if we're not careful we will have no hope, see no way of escape, and have no source of comfort.

The truth is that there **will be times** when we will feel down and out. But just because we may be DOWN doesn't mean that we have to be OUT.

Knocked down but we can get back up again. Why should we be so certain? Paul says because of the power of the Lord, we don't have to feel crushed or in despair, and we should know that we are not abandoned or destroyed.

Because of our relationship with the Lord, **when,** not if, trouble comes our way, we shouldn't become bitter, surprised, discouraged, or depressed nor should we give up or give in. Why? Because adversity is inevitable but you don't have to suffer amid adversity.

When Paul writes this 2nd letter to the church at Corinth, he knows that the church at Corinth has been through a season of great trials and difficulties. There were all kinds of attacks from outside the church and they had fears, discouragement, and anxiety on the inside.

Paul knew that when we are experiencing adversity; when we run to the right and there's a bear, and we run to the left and there's another bear – it's difficult to not get discouraged, to not be depressed, and to not give up. But how do you choose not to be discouraged and depressed when adversity strikes? First, recognize that there are many benefits to our experiencing adversity in our lives. James said that we should count it all joy when trouble, trials, and tribulations come into our lives because when our faith is tried, we are made stronger and able to handle the difficulties of life.

Furthermore, we should be encouraged when adversity strikes, because it allows us to see the power of the Lord. Think about Joseph who was hated by his brothers, sold into slavery, and later imprisoned but became second in control to the pharaoh.

Abraham was told by God to sacrifice his son, Isaac on a mountain area called Moriah, but God provided a ram in the bush. Moses and the children of Israel were trapped between the Red Sea and Pharoah's army but God made a highway of dry land to the other side. And Daniel and three Hebrew boys were thrown into deadly situations - a lion's den and a fiery furnace. But God turned deadly situations into death defying witnesses of His power.

In those situations, we are reminded that all adversity does not end in pain. Adversity shows us that God is all-powerful and that He is Real. Kenneth Morris penned the hymn, "Yes God is Real" in 1944,

> *"There are some things I may not know, there are some places I can't go. But I AM SURE of this one thing: my GOD IS REAL for I can feel Him deep within."*

Some folks may doubt, some folks may scorn, All can desert and leave me alone,

But as for me I'll take God's part For God is real and I can feel Him in my heart.

I cannot tell just how you felt When Jesus took your sins away, But since that day, yes, since that hour God has been real for I can feel His holy pow'r.

Yes, God is real, real in my soul, Yes, God is real for He has washed and made me whole; His love for me is like pure gold, Yes, God is real for I can feel Him in my soul.

I love the record in Mark 4:35 – 41 describing how Jesus and His disciples get into a boat to go to the other side of the Sea of Galilee and a storm comes up. Not a headache or a toothache but a situation that threatens their lives. A situation that they're helpless to control; a situation that creates emotional turmoil, that terrifies them; a situation that creates a spiritual, theological doubt – "Teacher, do you not care?"

Yes, you will have trouble but in the midst of your trouble, in the midst of your storm, there is one called Jesus who has overcome the world. He can give you peace in the middle of your storm and can strengthen you to overcome the pain of adversity.

You can have peace despite your adversity, if you are saved and realize that God is always at work in our lives, even during the most stressful circumstances. No matter how deep the valley, how troublesome your trial, or how difficult your trouble is, we can count on God. He said in His Holy Word:

- *"To not be anxious about anything, but in everything, by prayer and petition, with thanksgiving, present your requests to God. And the peace of God, which transcends all understanding, will guard your hearts and your minds in Christ Jesus."* (Philippians 4:6-7)
- *"No temptation, no trial, no struggle has overtaken you except what is common to mankind. And God is faithful; he will not let you be*

tempted beyond what you can bear. But when you are tempted, he will also provide a way out so that you can endure it." (1 Corinthians 10:13)

- *"All things work together for good for those who love God and the called according to His purpose."* (Romans 8:28)
- *"He will never leave you nor forsake you."* (Deuteronomy 31:8)
- *"God's grace is sufficient for you, for His power is made perfect in your weakness."* (2 Corinthians 12:9)
- And there was the psalmist who says amid our trials and tribulation, we should *"Lift up our eyes to the hills from whence cometh our help - All our help comes from the LORD, the Maker of heaven and earth."* (Psalm 121:1-2, KJV)

Paul summed it up this way in 2 Corinthians 4:16-18, *"Therefore, we do not lose heart. Though outwardly we are wasting away, yet inwardly we are being renewed day by day. For our light and momentary troubles are achieving for us an eternal glory that far outweighs them all. So we fix our eyes not on what is seen, but on what is unseen, since what is seen is temporary, but what is unseen is eternal."*

We have two choices when we face adversity – we can walk away from God, and the church; or we can walk into a deeper relationship with God. Since God is everywhere, even though you walk through the *"valley of the shadow of death, fear no evil because He is with you;"* (Psalm 23:4)

Since God is faithful, know that He will hear and answer prayer. Since God has all power, know that He is our refuge and strength, an ever-present help in trouble, and can calm every storm that may blow in our lives. So, when the storms of life and adversity, start your lifeboat to rocking and reeling, step out on faith and walk to Jesus.

When the storms of life are raging, know that you're still safe in the hands of Jesus who died . . . . and rose again. Some say that when they nailed Him to that cross He hit rock bottom or that he was on a dead-end street. But rock bottom can be solid ground and a dead-end street is a good place to turn around.

Just as Jesus rose, we can rise again every time we're knocked down. Proverbs 24:16 reminds us that *"the righteous man may fall seven times but he gets back up again."* Many of us have gone through some tough situations but we're still here today. Why? Because greater is He that is within us than he that is in the world.' (1 John 4:4)

Who is this "He" Who is within us? His name is Jesus! The lily of the valley . . . bright and morning star! Jesus, that "Hyperstatic Union" between the human and the divine! Two natures in one person unmixed forever. The Holy Spirit provided the divine and Mary provided the human. Throughout His life, we see these two natures. One minute he's thirsty, and the next He's walking on the water. One minute He says, "I hunger." And the next He's feeding thousands with a little boy's lunch. One minute He's dying on a cross and the next He's raising folks from the dead. It was asked, "What manner of man is this?" He's the only One who can feel it and fix it.

~

Life is not always absent of issues, trials, and struggles. The truth of the matter is that sometimes we can do everything right and life still goes wrong. In John 16:33, *Jesus said, "In the world we will have tribulation but be of good cheer, I have overcome the world."*

We will have situations of which we have no control; situations that create emotional turmoil within us; and if we're not careful, situations that cause us to question whether God cares about us. The bottom line is that we will experience adversity in life but we can have peace despite our adversity, if we are saved and realize that God is always at work in our lives, even during the most stressful circumstances.

REFLECTION QUESTIONS:

1. To not be overcome by adversity, reflect on these scriptures: Philippians 4:6-7; 1 Corinthians 10:13; Romans 8:28 and the 121st Psalm. What encouragement do you receive from them?
2. What will you do today, when adversity strikes?

CHAPTER 7

FROM HOPE TO DISAPPOINTMENT TO SATISFACTION

There was a man who got lost in the desert. After wandering around for a long time his throat became very dry, about that time he saw a little shack in the distance. He made his way over to the shack and found a water pump with a small jug of water and a note.

The note read: "Pour all the water into the top of the pump to prime it, if you do this you will get all the water you need". Now the man had a choice to make, if he trusted the note and poured the water in and it worked he would have all the water he needed. If it didn't work he would still be thirsty and he might die.

Or he could choose to drink the water in the jug and get immediate satisfaction, but it might not be enough and he still might die. After thinking about it the man decided to risk it. He poured the entire jug into the pump and began to work the handle, at first nothing happened and he got a little scared but he kept going and water started coming out. So much water came out that he drank all he wanted, took a shower, and filled all the containers he could find. Because he was willing to give up momentary satisfaction, he got all the water he needed. Now the note also said: after you have finished, please refill the jug for the next traveler." The man refilled the jug and added to the note: "Please prime the pump, believe me, it works"!

We have the same choice to make, do we hold on to what we have because we don't believe there are better things in store for us, and settle for immediate satisfaction? Or do we trust God and give up all that we have to get what God has promised us? I think the choice is obvious. We need to pour in all the water and trust God with everything. Then once we have experienced what God has to offer, the living water, we need to tell other people, "Go ahead prime the pump, believe me, it works"! (Contributed By: Randy Leckliter)

Each person experiences disappointments, the feeling of being let down, and dissatisfaction when something doesn't happen or turn out the way we expected it to, throughout life. In Luke 24:13-27 we see two of Jesus' followers who are experiencing disappointment.

> *"Now that same day two of them were going to a village called Emmaus, about seven miles from Jerusalem. They were talking with each other about everything that had happened. As they talked and discussed these things with each other, Jesus himself came up and walked along with them, but they were kept from recognizing him.*

> *He asked them, "What are you discussing together as you walk along?" They stood still, their faces downcast. One of them, named Cleopas, asked him, "Are you the only one visiting Jerusalem who does not know the things that have happened there in these days?" "What things?" he asked. "About Jesus of Nazareth," they replied. "He was a prophet, powerful in word and deed before God and all the people. The chief priests and our rulers handed him over to be sentenced to death, and they crucified Him, but we had hoped that he was the one who was going to redeem Israel. And what is more, it is the third day since all this took place. In addition, some of our women amazed us. They went to the tomb early this morning but didn't find his body. They came and told us that they had seen a vision of angels, who said he was alive. Then some of our companions went to the tomb and found it just as the women had said, but they did not see Jesus."*

He said to them, "How foolish you are, and how slow to believe all that the prophets have spoken! Did not the Messiah have to suffer these things and then enter his glory?" And beginning with Moses and all the Prophets, he explained to them what was said in all the Scriptures concerning himself."

These followers of Jesus were on their way to a place named Emmaus, their hometown. They had been to Jerusalem and were aware of the news of Jesus' death. As they walked along they were discussing the events that had happened on that "Same Day." That Jesus had been crucified, the following Sunday, women had found an empty tomb, and an angel had declared, *"He's not here."* (Matthew 28:6)

Well, Jesus was supposed to be the King, Savior, Messiah, and Deliverer. But He was crucified, died, and buried; and now they can't find Him. They were experiencing multiple emotions:

- Fear- If they can get to the Lord they can certainly get me.
- Anger- With the loss of their center of hope they would have been angry with God.
- Anxiety – What did the future hold for them?
- Frustration – The things that should have happened didn't happen like they should.
- Defeat – Their future of a changed world died with Jesus
- Hopelessness – Their hope was crushed with Jesus.
- Above all – DISAPPOINTMENT!

Have you ever been disappointed? There are probably some who struggle with disappointment. We are disappointed by people (marriage partners, work associates, friends). We get disappointed when our plans do not work out as we wanted (marriage, school, promotion). Sometimes we get disappointed with the twists of life (death, sickness, broken dreams).

The reality is that some disappointments are easier to handle than others. Some people recover quickly, while others get mired down in depression, and frustration, leading to stress, illness, and even death. Disappointment will enter all of our lives and all of us must be prepared to work through it.

The first thing we learn is that disappointment can close your eyes to the truth! Luke 23:15 – 16 tells us that the men were walking and talking and Jesus joined them but they did not recognize Him. Sometimes we're so preoccupied with ourselves, with our sorrow, with our situation that we don't recognize that Christ is with us. Well even though our eyes are blind to God, He not only sees but comes to us. We need to be reminded that David said in the 23rd Psalm that even in the valley of the shadow of death, God is with you. And the prophet said to "be strong and courageous. Do not be afraid or terrified because of them, for the Lord your God goes with you; He will never leave you nor forsake you." Consider the poem "Footprints in the Sand" by Mary Stevenson . . .

> One night I dreamed a dream.
> As I was walking along the beach with my Lord.
> Across the dark sky flashed scenes from my life.
> For each scene, I noticed two sets of footprints in the sand,
> One belonging to me and one to my Lord.
> After the last scene of my life flashed before me,
> I looked back at the footprints in the sand.
> I noticed that at many times along the path of my life,
> especially at the very lowest and saddest times,
> there was only one set of footprints.
> This really troubled me, so I asked the Lord about it.
> "Lord, you said once I decided to follow you,
> You'd walk with me all the way.
> But I noticed that during the saddest and most troublesome
> times of my life,
> there was only one set of footprints.
> I don't understand why, when I needed You the most, You
> would leave me."
> He whispered, "My precious child, I love you and will
> never leave you
> Never, ever, during your trials and tastings.
> When you saw only one set of footprints,
> It was then that I carried you."

As we face disappointments we need to be reminded that even though God does not shield his children from disappointment, we're never alone. When Jesus finds you in the midst of your trouble, He will accompany you and He will comfort you.

But don't be surprised if He also CONFRONTS you. In Luke 23, verses 17 – 27 – *Jesus asks, "What have you been talking about?" The men are incredulous that He hasn't heard about what happened to Jesus. After hearing their story Jesus says, "How foolish you are, and how slow to believe all that the prophets have spoken! Did not the Messiah have to suffer these things and then enter his glory?"*

Some things that disappoint us, happen for a reason, for a purpose, for God's purpose. Remember, James said, we should count it all as joy when we fall into diverse temptations, that the trying of your faith will make you stronger. (James 1:2-4) When we recognize that Jesus is with us during our times of disappointment, there will be a change in our demeanor, our attitudes, and our actions.

In Luke 23, verses 28-29, we see that as the men approached their village, Jesus was about to continue down the road but they invited Him to their home for dinner. Don't reject Jesus when trouble enters your life. Invite Him in!

If you invite Him in, He will come and sup with you. If He comes in, you'll find that He doesn't want to be served but wants to serve you. When He serves you something will happen. We see in verses Luke 23, 31 – 35 *that your eyes will be open to all around you; you'll recognize Jesus for Who He is; you'll get up and like Cleopas and the other, you'll have to go and tell somebody, "Did not our hearts burn as He opened the scriptures to us."*

Finally, disappointment has the potential to cause you to lose hope. That is the fundamental meaning behind this passage of scripture found in Luke 23. The disciples had lost hope and were going home with their heads hung low.

Disappointment causes frustration. Jesus called the disciples "foolish ones." This frustration can drive us to do things we would never do otherwise. But it is not the disappointment but the handling of the disappointment that matters. The most important thing is to handle our disappointment with God's help.

I want you to know that Jesus can transform defeat into victory. He can change sadness into singing. He can change darkness into light. And He can change bitterness into sweetness. He can change disappointment into good news.

You may be struggling with an impossible feeling that cannot be overcome. Your words may be "I cannot do this." That is exactly the point. You cannot but Jesus can. Jesus can transform the trial into a victory. When Jesus shows up, disappointments blow up.

The presence of Jesus reveals God's plan and God's plans cannot be frustrated nor can they be defeated. Isaiah 54:17 tells us that *"No weapon formed against you, shall prosper."* The presence of Jesus in your life gives new hope and meaning. When you have hope you're willing to get up and do something. The disciples on the road to Emmaus got up and were motivated to serve. These two disciples are walking that Resurrection morning, that morning when death was defeated. But instead of rejoicing that day, they are running away.

We should not lose sight of the source of our hope – Jesus. The One who died for the world on Calvary.

⁓

God is always at work in our lives, even during the worst of times. Romans 8:28 tells us that *"All things work together for the good of those who love the Lord and are the called according to His purpose."* So don't forget the One who provides for you, the One who saved you.

REFLECTION QUESTIONS:

1. When was the last time God came through for you? Have you thanked Him enough for what He did?
2. Do you believe that in your times of trouble, you can count on God? Here are a few scriptures that confirm that you can. Reflect on 2 Peter 3:9; 1 Corinthians 15:58; Isaiah 40:30-31; Jeremiah 29:11; 2 Corinthians 4:16-18; and Philippians 4:6–7.

CHAPTER 8

OVERCOMING TEMPTATION

According to the website, Preaching Today (www.preachingtoday.com), phishing is a word for a type of online scamming which is growing. The FBI reports over 300,000 complaints and over 50 million dollars in phishing losses in 2022.

Phishing occurs when someone sends you a bogus communication, usually by email or text message, disguised as a missive from a legitimate source, such as a bank or government agency. Usually, the sender is angling for information, a credit card number, or a transfer of funds. Sometimes there is an attachment containing malware or a link where you can go to log in—which is to say, to have your password stolen.

Phishing grows and grows, demanding continual vigilance; billions of phishing emails are sent every day, some narrowly targeted and others broadcast widely. You have no doubt seen the con artists' bait dangling in your inbox.

Phishing has some similarities to the kind of temptations Christians encounter. Every Christian is aware of the temptations of the world and what could happen if we are baited, hooked, and reeled in. An example of phishing is found in Matthew 4:1 – 11 where Jesus is tempted.

> *Then Jesus was led by the Spirit into the wilderness to be tempted by the devil. ² After fasting forty days and forty nights, he was hungry. ³ The tempter came to him and said, "If you are the Son of God, tell these stones to become bread."*

⁴ Jesus answered, "It is written: 'Man shall not live on bread alone, but on every word that comes from the mouth of God.'"

⁵ Then the devil took him to the holy city and had him stand on the highest point of the temple. ⁶ "If you are the Son of God," he said, "throw yourself down. For it is written: "'He will command his angels concerning you, and they will lift you up in their hands, so that you will not strike your foot against a stone.'" ⁷ Jesus answered him, "It is also written: 'Do not put the Lord your God to the test.'" ⁸ Again, the devil took him to a very high mountain and showed him all the kingdoms of the world and their splendor. ⁹ "All this I will give you," he said, "if you will bow down and worship me." ¹⁰ Jesus said to him, "Away from me, Satan! For it is written: Worship the Lord your God, and serve him only.'" ¹¹ Then the devil left him, and angels came and attended him.

Temptations will come our way, and if we are not careful, we will yield to them, and be defeated because we have yielded and yielding is sin. Let me ask you, did you yield to temptation last night? This morning? What bait does Satan use against you? Lust, pornography, drugs, gambling, alcohol, shopping for stuff, jewelry?

It is not a matter of what are you going do if you are tempted, it's what are you going to do **when** you are tempted. Satan might not be using the bait to hook you that he was using yesterday but like a good fisherman, if the fish aren't biting one bait, he'll change to another bait.

In Matthew's record of the temptation of Jesus, we see Satan use several of his tactics and tricks to tempt Jesus. But Jesus doesn't yield and we don't have to yield either. If we understand Satan's tactics and follow Jesus' example, we can resist the wiles of the devil and have victory over temptation. Let's consider a few of Satan's tactics.

Satan's first tactic is to always look for the right conditions to attack. He will attack either when you're up or when you're down – he is so good at picking the most interesting times to tempt us. Jesus began His ministry by having John the Baptist, baptize Him and immediately afterward Jesus was led into the wilderness to be tempted.

When you're trying to do your best – when you give your life to Christ – when you've recommitted yourself to the Lord – when you've decided to lead a new ministry, look out for trouble. Never become too comfortable. Just because you've won one battle, doesn't mean you've won the war. In the book of Job, Satan was asked where he had been and his response was, "I've been walking to and fro in the earth seeking who I might destroy." (Job 1:7) Don't let your guard down; don't go to sleep. Be ye ever ready. If Satan will attack Jesus, know that he will go after you.

Satan's second strategy is to attack you physically – through lusts or desires of the flesh. Matthew tells us that Jesus had spent 40 days fasting in the Judean wilderness where the heat made His hunger and thirst even greater. So, after 40 days in such a place, it is an understatement when Matthew says that Jesus "hungered." He was starving.

And now this sudden, severe hunger became the opportunity for Satan's first temptation. He said to Jesus, "If thou be the Son of God, command that these stones be made bread." Now there is nothing wrong with Jesus turning stone to bread. The gospel record tells us that later He would change water into wine, and multiply a few loaves and fishes to feed thousands.

So, He had the power to change stones into bread. The problem is that turning stones into bread was outside of the will of God. God's will is that we trust and depend on Him. God's will is that we satisfy our desires in the right way. Yes, we need food, but we don't have to overeat. Yes, sexual relations were created by God but it was designed for marriage.

Satan will tailor his temptation to you as an individual and do his best to convince you that it is ok to operate outside the will of God. Whatever you're hungering for, that's what you'll be faced with. And when we are hungry, not just hungry for food, but hungry for a loving relationship, hungry for something to comfort us when we're feeling all alone, hungry for something to ease the pain of a broken relationship, hungry for something to give you peace amid a storm, you are ripe for temptation. And Satan will attack you when you're hungry.

Well, if you are hungry, listen to Jesus' response to Satan's first attack. He quoted Deuteronomy 8:3 (KJV), *"Man doth not live by bread only, but by every word that proceedeth out of the mouth of the LORD."* That tells us that temptation can be resisted by scripture because the Word of God is the weapon Satan fears more than anything else in this world. 2 Timothy

3:16-17 tells us that *"All Scripture is God-breathed and is useful for teaching, rebuking, correcting and training in righteousness, so that the servant of God may be thoroughly equipped for every good work."*

The Word of God is also part of your Christian Armor. Ephesians 6:11-17 tells us to *"put on the whole armor of God, that ye may be able to stand against the wiles of the devil. For we wrestle not against flesh and blood, but against principalities, against powers, against the rulers of the darkness of this world, against spiritual wickedness in high places. Therefore, put on the whole armor of God, that you may be able to withstand in the evil day, and having done all, to stand. And take the...sword of the Spirit, which is the word of God."*

As the Son of God, Jesus was obeying His Father to go into the wilderness, and Jesus knew that His Father would provide for His every need. Jesus trusted in the provision of God just the same way we have to trust in the provision of God. Jesus tells us in Matthew 6:33 that we should *"seek first the kingdom of God and his righteousness, and all these things shall be added unto you."*

So, don't let Satan defeat you through lusts of the flesh. Know that God will satisfy your hunger, he will meet your needs, just wait on the Lord and He will take care of your every need.

In Matthew 4:5-7, we see Satan's next tactic where he attacks us mentally and emotionally. *Satan took Jesus to the top of the temple and said, "So, you trust your Father? Well, let's see how much you trust Him because if you won't work a miracle for yourself, then let's see if God will work one for you. And since you seem to know Scripture, let me give you one,"* and Satan quotes Psalm 91:11-12 and says, *"For it is written: 'He will command his angels concerning you, and they will lift you up in their hands so that you will not strike your foot against a stone.'* In other words, Satan was tempting Christ to prove the reality of God's love and care.

Satan was hoping that Jesus would leap and God would not honor Jesus' trust, and the Messiah would fall upon the rocks below and die. That would end God's plan of salvation. But Jesus' response was to again quote from the scriptures. Quoting Deuteronomy 6:16 *Jesus says, "Do not put the Lord your God to the test."*

My brothers and sisters Satan will use the Word of God against you if he can. In this situation, he's tempting Jesus to act not on faith but on His will. He will try to get us to do the same thing.

Imagine that you're driving 90 miles per hour on a residential street, running through every red light and stop sign, and you say, "I have faith that God will protect me." And then you crash and kill yourself and others. Someone may say you died in faith, but I would say you died putting God to the test.

Satan will tempt you to do foolish things and demand that God deliver you from the result of your foolish actions. Yes, sometimes in His mercy and grace, God will take care of the fool, but you can't expect it or demand it.

Returning to the temptation of Christ, we see that since Satan has failed in his first two attempts to conquer his enemy, we see Satan's third tactic, which is to attack us through our pride, and our ego. In Matthew 4:8 Satan shows Jesus all the kingdoms of the world and tells Him "You can have it all, if you will only bow down and worship me."

Satan knew Jesus was promised the kingdom and that that kingdom would be received only after a three and one-half-year ministry that concluded with suffering and dying on the cross. So Satan tempts Him to accept a kingdom now. All Jesus had to do was to bow down and worship Satan who offered Jesus a shortcut. Jesus could enjoy all the glory and power now, and not have to go through any suffering.

Well, Satan effectively uses that same temptation today – it's called instant gratification. Too many are like Esau, who traded the value of his birthright for the temporary pleasure of a meal. Instead, we need to follow the example of Christ. He remained loyal to God and went on to endure the pain and suffering of an old rugged cross. He did so because He knew that beyond the cross, was a crown of glory.

Again, in response to Satan's third temptation, Jesus demonstrates that the word of God is our best defense. He quotes Exodus 20:3, *"You shall have no other gods before Me."* In other words, Christ is telling us to put God and our obedience to Him above everything else. Your life will be a lot less complicated if you will just Trust in the LORD with all thine heart; and lean not unto thine own understanding. *In all thy ways acknowledge him, and he shall direct thy paths."* (Proverbs 3:5-6)

If you are a Christian, Satan has no authority over you. Paul wrote in 1 Corinthians 10:13 *"There hath no temptation taken you but such as is* common to man: but God is faithful, who will not suffer you to be tempted above that ye are able; but will with the temptation also make a way to escape, that ye may be able to bear it."

So, we see in Matthew 4:11 that the battle was over, *"Satan left Jesus and angels came and ministered to Him."* Likewise, after you've gone through the fire, there is a time of celebration, a time of blessing. Everything you're going through; every temptation is just for a season – *"weeping may endure for a night but joy comes in the morning."* (Psalm 30:5)

Satan tried to win the war for you and me by attacking Jesus physically, then mentally, and finally, spiritually. He used the lust of the flesh, the lust of the eyes, and the pride of life to tempt Jesus just as he uses them to tempt us today. But let me remind you that whatever you're going through, all things work together for the good of those who love the Lord and are called according to His purpose. (Romans 8:28)

I am also reminded that we must be persuaded that *"in all these things we are more than conquerors through him that loved us."* (Romans 8:38-39) It doesn't matter what you're going through – Jesus can bring peace amid a storm. We must be persuaded that . . .

- "That neither death, nor life, nor angels, nor principalities, nor powers, nor things present, nor things to come, Nor height, nor depth, nor any other creature, shall be able to separate us from the love of God, which is in Christ Jesus our Lord.
- to stay on this battlefield even if it looks like you are at the end of your road.
- When I walk through the valley of the shadow of death, it's not the end of the road, cause the Lord is with me.
- When I have nothing you will still supply my every need.
- When my enemy is on top, I will be still and let the Lord fight my battle
- When I'm weak, greater is He that is in me, than he who is in the world
- No weapon formed against me shall prosper
- If we confess our sins, he is faithful and just and will forgive us our sins and purify us from all unrighteousness.

Let me also remind you that Judas thought his betrayal was the end of the road but he later discovered it was only a bend. Jews who thought trading Jesus for Barabas was the end of the road but it was only a bend. Roman soldiers thought nailing Him to the cross was the end of the road but it was only a bend. When Jesus hung His head and said "It is finished", Satan thought it was the end of the road but it was only a bend. When they rolled a stone in the doorway of that borrowed tomb, they thought it was the end, but it was only a bend.

Christ won the victory not just in the desert but on Calvary's cross. Jesus offered up Himself as a sacrifice for sin, yours and mine.

༄

It has been said that small things matter because small things may lead to larger things. And sometimes those larger things result in painful consequences. In Genesis 3:6, Eve "saw" the forbidden fruit. No sin but she "desired." She had the opportunity to sin and therefore was tempted but no sin. Then she "took and ate." Sin. As written in James 1:15, after desire has (been) conceived, it gives birth to sin." The "look" seemed harmless. It was a small thing, but it led to "eating." And as James also said, "when it (sin) is full-grown, it gives birth to death."

REFLECTION QUESTIONS:

1. Desire and opportunity lead to temptation. Are there things in your life that you are "looking" at (desire)? Things that seem harmless now, but could lead to larger things?
2. Since sin occurs when we yield to temptation; and desire begins with the things we look at, the things we think about; what thoughts do you need to "take captive" (2 Corinthians 10:5)? What things do you think about that do not give honor and praise to God (Philippians 4:8)?

Remember that Satan is always on the prowl, so *"Watch and pray, lest you enter into temptation. The spirit indeed is willing, but the flesh is weak."* (Matthew 26:41)

CHAPTER 9

SHAKE OFF THE VIPERS IN YOUR LIFE

The only survivor of a shipwreck was washed up on a small, uninhabited island. He prayed feverishly for God to rescue him, and every day he scanned the horizon for help, but none came.

Exhausted, he eventually managed to build a little hut out of driftwood as a shelter and a place to store his few remaining possessions. One day, after scavenging for food, he arrived home to find his little hut in flames, the smoke rolling up to the sky. Everything was lost. Stunned with grief and anger, he cried, "God, how could you do this to me!"

Early the next day, however, he was awakened by the sound of a ship approaching the island. It had come to rescue him. "How did you know I was here?" the weary man asked. "We saw your smoke signal," they replied.

God is always at work in our lives, even during the most stress-filled circumstances. When we trust in the Lord with everything we are and everything we have, when we depend upon his truth instead of our understanding and choose to walk in obedience, God promises to *"make our paths straight"* (Proverbs 3:6).

The Apostle Paul was in the center of God's perfect will. He had been threatened with death in the city of Jerusalem …. but he was in God's perfect will. He had been arrested by the Romans…. but he was in God's perfect will. He had been locked away in a dark damp cell…. but he was in God's perfect will.

He was bound and escorted under guard to a ship that would take him to his final destination, a place from which there would be no coming back,…. but he was in God's perfect will. He was held prisoner among heathen sailors who cared little for God,…. but he was in God's perfect will. He was on a ship bound for Rome…. a ship that would face one of the fiercest storms in Biblical times… a ship that would be broken into many small pieces, shipwrecked on a strange island, … but he was still in God's perfect will. This event in Paul's life is described in Acts 28:1 – 6.

"Once safely on shore, we found out that the island was called Malta. The islanders showed us unusual kindness. They built a fire and welcomed us all because it was raining and cold. Paul gathered a pile of brushwood and, as he put it on the fire, a viper, driven out by the heat, fastened itself on his hand. When the islanders saw the snake hanging from his hand, they said to each other, "This man must be a murderer; for though he escaped from the sea, the goddess Justice has not allowed him to live." But Paul shook the snake off into the fire and suffered no ill effects. The people expected him to swell up or suddenly fall dead; but after waiting a long time and seeing nothing unusual happen to him, they changed their minds and said he was a god."

Like the shipwreck survivor who was rescued as a result of divine providence, Paul finds himself on an island after suffering through a shipwreck. Just because we go through adversities, storms of life, and the attacks of the principalities and evil deeds…. this does not mean that we are not in God's perfect will.

Many times, it's exactly the opposite. All along this road of life that we all must travel there will be pitfalls…., troubles…., trials and tribulations…. that we cannot avoid. Yes, unexpected tragedies will slow down our progress, alter our plans, and give us great frustration. Our best plans will be shattered by the circumstances of life and we may find ourselves shipwrecked but we are still in God's perfect will.

Now on this island, Paul and his companions are met by natives who built a fire for them. Paul gets more wood for the fire and the heat drives out a viper from within the wood and it bites Paul on the hand. We must understand what we're dealing with when we refer to vipers. Satan was the snake, the viper, and Paul's ministry stirred up the viper.

Two things happened here that made the serpent mad. First, the weather was cold and the serpent, a cold-blooded animal, was nearly frozen, hiding from view in the wood. But somebody started a fire and the viper started to warm it up.

That tells us that Satan won't bother you if you are cold in the Lord. He doesn't care what we do as long, as we don't work for the Lord. But if we stir up the fire and let the Holy Ghost move..... look out... THE SNAKES WILL START TO MOVE!

Second, after a fire has been started, more wood is needed to keep the fire burning. Let me tell you that the more you pray, the more you give the Lord the Praise, and the more you obey God's Holy Word, the more you can expect Satan to move against you. And he will attack when you least expect it.

Next notice that the viper didn't attack and let go of Paul. It struck and held on. Do you sometimes feel like the attack of the devil in your life is never going to end? That Satan just won't turn loose? That's when you need to do what Paul did and just shake it off.

We also need to remember that Isaiah 54:17 reminded us that, *"No weapon that is formed against thee shall prosper."* God wants you to stay on the course and finish the race that is set before you. The attacks will come but the victory is yours already.

During the 1968 Olympic Games in Mexico City, the crowd started to leave the Olympic Stadium after the 10,000-meter race. Then the crowd stopped when they saw one lone runner on the home stretch. He would be the very last one to cross the finish line.

It was a runner from the little country of Tanzania, Africa. But he wasn't running to the finish line, he was limping into the stadium because of an injured leg. As he struggled, the medics tried to help, but he waved them back.

He finally crossed the finish line and collapsed, too weak to get up on his own. When the medics asked why he kept running despite his injury,

He said, "My country didn't send me 7,000 miles to start the race. They sent me 7,000 miles to finish the race!"

If we're going to finish this Christian race, we have to Shake the Devil Off. We should never give up! And then like Apostle Paul, we'll be able to say, *"I HAVE FOUGHT A GOOD FIGHT.... I HAVE FINISHED MY COURSE... I HAVE KEPT THE FAITH."* (2 Timothy 4:7-8 KJV)

But the race is difficult because vipers often appear in the fires of life – having difficulty, feeling vulnerable, or weak? Look out - some snake in the grass or wood pile will put a sneak attack on you.

What's important is that it's not the snake but the venom that will do the most harm including killing you. What kind of venom does Satan have? How about self-destruction, depression, hatred, sadness, confusion, impatience, anger, unfaithfulness, unkindness, unforgiveness, harshness, lack of self-control, and hatred? It's all venom! All poison.

But like Paul, we need to shake off the vipers of discouragement, criticism, and cynicism. In the 3rd verse, we see that Paul was attacked while helping, trying to do good – gathering wood. Vipers will often appear when you're doing your best for the Lord. Paul could have allowed this attack to discourage him; he could have said – *"Lord you brought me through some angry and stormy seas just to die of a snake bite on this lonely island."* But no, Paul shook it off. He remembered God's promises – *"I'll never leave you nor forsake you."* (Hebrews 13:5)

Like Paul, we need to shake off the viper of criticism. In Acts 28:4 we see that after Paul was snake bitten, those around him began to whisper and murmur – *"No doubt this man is a murderer."* When you're doing your best, trying to do good, know that some around you will be quick to judge, criticize, and falsely accuse you. Don't be surprised but be careful because if you are not careful, criticism will make you want to give up and quit. So when the viper of criticism attacks, just look to Jesus the author and finisher of our faith, and shak'em off!"

Finally, like Paul, we need to shake off the vipers of cynicism. Acts 28:6 tells us *"The people around Paul, after seeing him bitten by the viper, expected him to swell up or suddenly fall dead,"* They looked for nothing good to come of this situation.

Have you been the object of a cynic's words? The cynic is the one who has nothing but low expectations of you as a Christian. When you try something new or difficult, the cynic looks at you and your situation and says, *"You will never make it. This church thing won't last. You will fail. You will fall. This isn't real!"* *"I told you so."* I want you to know that no cynic has the last word, God does!

As a shepherd boy, David had his cynics when he said that he would go and fight the giant Philistine. *King Saul said, "You're only a boy and he's been a warrior since he was a boy."* (Jeremiah 1:7)

So, what did David do? He shook off the viper of cynicism and proved the doubters wrong.

Shake off their low opinion of you by looking to the one who sits high and looks low. Look to the One who caused Paul to write – *"I can do all things through Christ Jesus, who strengthens me."* (Philippians 4:13)

Look to the one who said, "I'll never leave you, nor forsake you." (Deuteronomy 31:8b) With your eyes on Jesus, tell yourself, "I'm shaking them off!"

The end of Acts 28:6 tells us that, *"after waiting a long time and seeing nothing unusual happen to him, they (the islanders) changed their minds and said he was a god."* Well, Paul knew that he wasn't a god but he served a great God.

You can shake the vipers off, if you remember the words of the Psalmist who said, *"The LORD is my light and my salvation; whom shall I fear? The LORD is the **strength** of my life; of whom shall I be afraid?"* (Psalm 27:1)

You can shake it off if you keep your eyes on Calvary and the one who gave His life for you and me. His name is Jesus!

One of Satan's strategies is to convince us to compromise our beliefs. Compromise is an interesting word. On the surface, it sounds like a reasonable action to take; in negotiations, it is one way to reach an agreement or settle differences. One of the interesting things about compromise is that each side has to give up something. That may be ok when you're negotiating financial matters such as the purchase of a house or car. However, when the objective of the compromise is to give up our values, our principles, our beliefs, or our integrity, the process of sin has begun.

Daniel didn't compromise by taking the easy way out. Because he knew that the consequences of compromise led to death. Therefore, we are to "Be strong and of a good courage; be not afraid, neither be dismayed for the Lord thy God is with you, wherever you go." (Joshua 1:9)

That's why Christianity without commitment is Christianity without Christ. And in this Christian Walk, there is nothing positive about the word or the act of Compromise.

REFLECTION QUESTIONS:

1. If you are going to be committed and not compromise, you have to dare to be different. What areas of your life are you challenged to compromise?

2. In addition, it is not the public decisions that determine the quality of our faith, it's the private ones. Talk to the Lord about His help in dealing with those private times when you compromise His Word and His Way.

CHAPTER 10

GOD WILL WORK IT OUT

From "The Seed" (Author Unknown) – A successful Christian businessman was growing old and knew it was time to choose a successor to take over the business. He called all the young executives in his company together. He said, "It is time for me to step down and choose the next CEO. I have decided to choose one of you."

The young executives were shocked, but the boss continued. "I am going to give each one of you a SEED today—one very special SEED. I want you to plant the seed, water it, and come back here one year from today with what you have grown from the seed I have given you. I will then judge the plants that you bring, and the one I choose will be the next CEO."

One man, named Jim, was there that day and he, like the others, received a seed. He went home and excitedly, told his wife the story. She helped him get a pot, soil, and compost, and he planted the seed. Everyday he would water it and watch to see if it had grown.

After about three weeks, some of the other executives began to talk about their seeds and the plants that were beginning to grow. Jim kept checking his seed, but nothing ever grew. Three weeks, four weeks, five weeks went by, but still nothing. By now others were talking about their plants, but Jim didn't have a plant and he felt like a failure.

Six months went by—still nothing in Jim's pot. He just knew he had killed his seed. Everyone else had trees and tall plants, but he had nothing. Jim didn't say anything to his colleagues, however. He just kept watering and fertilizing the soil—He so wanted the seed to grow.

A year finally went by and all the young executives of the company brought their plants to the CEO for inspection. Jim told his wife that he wasn't going to take an empty pot. But she asked him to be honest about what happened. Jim felt sick at his stomach. It was going to be the most embarrassing moment of his life, but he knew his wife was right.

He took his empty pot to the board room. When Jim arrived, he was amazed at the variety of plants grown by the other executives. They were beautiful—in all shapes and sizes. Jim put his empty pot on the floor and many of his colleagues laughed. A few felt sorry for him!

When the CEO arrived, he surveyed the room and greeted his young executives. Jim just tried to hide in the back. "My, what great plants, trees, and flowers you have grown," said the CEO. "Today one of you will be appointed the next CEO!" All of a sudden, the CEO spotted Jim at the back of the room with his empty pot. He ordered the financial director to bring him to the front. Jim was terrified. He thought, "The CEO knows I'm a failure! Maybe he will have me fired!" When Jim got to the front, the CEO asked him what had happened to his seed—Jim told him the story.

The CEO asked everyone to sit down except Jim. He looked at Jim, and then announced to the young executives, "Behold, your next Chief Executive! His name is Jim!" Jim couldn't believe it. Jim couldn't even grow his seed! How could he be the new CEO the others said?

Then the CEO said, "One year ago today, I gave everyone in this room a seed. I told you to take the seed, plant it, water it, and bring it back to me today. But I gave you all boiled seeds; they were dead—it was not possible for them to grow. All of you, except Jim, have brought me trees and plants and flowers. When you found that the seed would not grow, you substituted another seed for the one I gave you. Jim was the only one with the courage and honesty to bring me a pot with my seed in it. Therefore, he is the one who will be the new Chief Executive!"

In Romans 8:28 Paul writes of something that we should learn and know. He said, *"And we know that in all things God works for the good of those who love him, who have been called according to his purpose."*

This is awesome news for everyone who loves God. Paul essentially says that everything that happened to you in the past, everything that is happening to you today, and everything that will happen to you in the future, God has been working, God is working now, and God will be working it out for your present and eternal good. That is a promise that you should believe with certainty and completeness.

Paul says, "We know this." Paul doesn't say, "It would be wonderful if in all things God is working for our good." He doesn't say, "Let's pretend they do . . . let's imagine it . . . let's hope that this is so." Paul says with certainty and conviction, "Know this: God is ceaselessly, energetically, and purposefully active on your behalf."

Paul knew what it was like for a follower of Christ to have moments when they question their faith. Have you had any momentary doubts? Rain just keeps falling in your life and you find yourself asking, "Lord did you forget about me?"

Yes, we all have moments when we wonder whether the problems will stop, whether the issues will go away and whether we will have a moment of peace in our life. But Paul says in our text that you can be certain that whatever you're going through, **know that** God will work it out. Are you a witness to God working it out for you?

Well, you may be asking "Why is Paul so certain?" Let me acknowledge that the purpose of things that happen is not always good to us. We make some bad choices all by ourselves.

Let me also say that the God we serve is omniscient – He knows all. Therefore, God never shakes his head in wonder saying, "I never knew that that was going to happen." But those who love God, who responded to His call, who accepted His gift of grace through Jesus Christ, will reap benefits in all things and all situations – whether we consider those situations good or bad. James went so far as to tell us in 1:2-4, *"My brethren, count it all joy when you fall into various trials, 3 knowing that the testing of your faith produces patience. 4 But let patience have its perfect work, that you may be perfect and complete, lacking nothing."*

That should give someone some comfort but you may be wondering just how that can be asserted. Well, I didn't, God did. Again, Paul wrote in Romans 8:28, *"In all things God works for the good of those who love him."*

Consider Job and his afflictions – Satan's purpose was to break him to show God that he wasn't all that faithful. Not only did Job have material wealth returned to him, but every preacher still uses his example to encourage their congregation to hang in there. God will always work it out.

Joseph was sold into slavery, and placed in jail – years later was the source of food and safety for his family during a time of famine. God will always work it out.

While other Hebrew baby boys were being slaughtered, Moses was placed in a river, lived outside of his mother's home, later sent into the wilderness for killing an Egyptian overseer. But God wasn't through with him, later God used Moses to free his people and take them to the Promised Land. God will always work it out.

Unfortunately, we sometimes let our circumstances blind us to the truth that God will always work it out. How does this happen? Well, we're all traveling down life's highway. Smooth sailing is what we prefer. Straight ways - No potholes in the road. All downhill - No strain, no Stress. We can turn on the cruise control, and maybe even the autopilot if we own a self-driving car.

But there are times when we find ourselves approaching a bend in the road. If we're not careful those bends in the road will look like the end of the road. Likewise, there are times when we're traveling, and we encounter bad weather – heavy rain, fog, blowing snow and you just can't see your way. It takes a different kind of driving to drive in bad weather or to get through a bend or curve in the road, than it does to drive on a straight, smooth road.

The same is true on the road of life – when we can't see our way, to see beyond the bends, we first have to have started our journey by stopping in at God's service station – get our tanks filled with the Holy Spirit and have Jesus as our driver.

Then we have to commit ourselves to seeing our journey to the very end. As Paul wrote in Philippians 3:14, *"I press toward the mark for the prize of the high calling of God in Christ Jesus."*

But too often in life, we find ourselves at a point where we don't think we can go any further. So many bad things are happening to us; it feels like we just can't go on, that's when we need to **let faith take over**. Hebrews 11:1 tells us that "faith is the substance of things hoped for, the evidence of things not seen." I see what looks like a bad bend in the road, but God told me that He would see me through; I can't see the end of the road, but God told me if I would just trust Him, everything will be all right.

I need to be like those airplane pilots who fly at night or in heavy fog. When I can't see my way, I'm going to turn it over, not to my autopilot, but to my master pilot – Captain Jesus, the author and finisher of our faith.

Second, to get through the bends of life, we need to be Obedient to God's word. Have you noticed those signs before and during bends in the road? No words, just pictures that tell you the curve is coming up. The sign will tell you what kind of curve (gradual, right hand, or hairpin) and will tell you the proper speed to safely negotiate the curve. If you're obedient to those rules, you won't have too much trouble getting through the bend in the road.

Likewise, God's given us some rules to follow in every life situation we face. Love the Lord your God with all your heart, soul, and mind & neighbor as yourself. Remember the Sabbath day, to keep it holy. - Honor your father and your mother. Seek ye first the kingdom of God, & his righteousness; & all these things shall be added unto you.

To negotiate the curves of life, to know God's rules for the bends in the road of life, we must first *"study to show thyself approved unto God, a workman that needeth not to be ashamed, rightly dividing the word of truth."* (2 Timothy 2:15) But just knowing the rules of the road won't help you to stay safe if you aren't willing to obey them. You may get by for a while (no accidents and no tickets). But sooner or later, the road will get rough and the hills will be hard to climb. That's why the prophet Isaiah 1: 19-20 tells us, *"If you are willing and obedient, you will eat the good things of the land; but if you resist and rebel, you will be devoured by the sword."*

This leads to the third aspect of our driving which is critical to negotiating bends in the road. We must be patient! Consider taking a bend or curve in the road at too great a speed. You'll either flip over or skid off the road. We too often want to get through difficult situations as fast as we can; we want the unpleasantness over, no more bad memories, no more issues with the people; we won't the pain and suffering to cease.

But Isaiah 40:31 tells us that *"they that wait upon the LORD shall renew their strength; they shall mount up with wings as eagles; they shall run, and not be weary; and they shall walk, and not faint."* To get through the difficulties of life, Isaiah says you have to be patient.

Finally, Paul says in Romans 8:28 *"All things work together for good."* But what is the "good" he is talking about? It's not a better set of circumstances like health, happiness, money, or a nice place to live.

The "good" that Paul is speaking about here is shared with us in the remaining verses of this chapter where he tells us that God knew us before we were born. That God knew who would accept His gift of salvation through faith in Jesus. That God gives life and life more abundantly to those who trust in Jesus. Most importantly the good that all things are working together is to make us like Jesus. And there is no higher good than to be like the Lord Jesus Christ.

Paul goes on to tell us we must be persuaded that *"in all these things we are more than conquerors through him that loved us."* (Romans 8:37) To be persuaded means to be convinced to not just believe but to act on our belief. So, my brothers and sisters, I want to persuade you that no matter what you're going through – Jesus can bring peace in the midst of a storm. Amen?

Paul says *We must be persuaded that "that neither death, nor life, nor angels, nor principalities, nor powers, nor things present, nor things to come, nor height, nor depth, nor any other creature, shall be able to separate us from the love of God, which is in Christ Jesus our Lord."* (Romans 8:38-39)

Sometimes we feel like God has left us but we must be persuaded that No weapon formed against us shall prosper and that as the prophet said, "God will never leave us nor forsake us."

When it looks like you are at the end of your road, be persuaded to stay on this battlefield. What did the songwriter say, "I'm on the battlefield for my Lord. I promised Him that I would serve Him till I die."

So be persuaded that . . .

- When we walk through the valley of the shadow of death, it's not the end of the road, because the Lord is with us;
- When we have nothing, the Lord will still supply our every need;
- When our enemy is on top, just be still and let the Lord fight your battle;
- When you're feeling weak, just remember that greater is He that is in you, than he who is in the world (1 John 4:4); and
- If we confess our sins, He is faithful and just and will forgive us our sins and purify us from all unrighteousness. (1 John 1:9)

Interestingly, we're not the only ones who thought a bend in the road was the end of the road . . .

- Jews thought trading Jesus for Barabas was the end of the road but it was only a bend;
- Roman soldiers thought nailing Him to the cross was the end of the road but it was only a bend;
- When Jesus hung His head and said "It is finished", Satan thought it was the end of the road but it was only a bend;
- When they rolled a stone in the doorway of that borrowed tomb, they thought it was the end, but it was only a bend.

Early on Sunday morning, the Rock that was put inside of a rock . . .and He got up with all power in His Holy and Righteous Hands. That's why I'm persuaded that as long as I've got King Jesus, everything will be alright.

In the 43rd chapter of Isaiah, the prophet reassures the captive nation of Israel and each of us that God is our creator, our Lord, our Redeemer, and the Holy One who keeps His promises. We can reflect on God's blessings in the past where a way was made out of what seemed to be no way.

When I consider the amazing baking skills of my mother, I remember her making pound cakes from scratch. The ingredients, Flour, salt, vanilla, baking powder, and eggs by themselves, did not taste good. However, when mixed in the right proportions, sweetened with sugar (and love), and then subjected to the heat of an oven, produced a cake to "die for." Likewise, God takes the distasteful things in our lives, mixes them in the right proportions, and after subjecting us to the right amount of life pressure, produces good in us.

REFLECTION QUESTIONS:

1. Can you recall a life situation that initially was unpleasant but you later benefited from?
2. Is there someone in your life who can be encouraged by the life lessons that you have learned? If so, share it with them today.

CHAPTER 11

YOUR ROCK IN A HARD PLACE

There was a weak, sickly man who lived in the deep back woods in an old log cabin. In front of his cabin was a huge boulder. One night in a dream the man heard a voice tell him to go out there and push the huge rock all day long, day after day. The man got up early in the morning, and with great excitement, he pushed the rock until lunch, then he rested a while and pushed the rock until supper time. The man loved pushing against the rock, it gave his life meaning.

The dream was so real that it was with great excitement that he pushed against the rock. Day after day he pushed. As days rolled into weeks, and weeks into months, he faithfully pushed against the rock.

After 8 months of pushing the rock, the man tired of pushing the rock and in his tiredness, he started to doubt his dream. So, one day he measured from his porch to the rock, and after daily pushing the rock, he would measure to see how much he had moved the rock. After two weeks of pushing and measuring, he realized he had not moved the rock a fraction of an inch. As a matter of fact, the boulder was in the same place as when he started.

The man was disappointed because he thought the dream was special but now after 9 months he saw his work had accomplished nothing. He sat on his porch and cried and cried, he had invested many hundred hours into nothing.

As the sun was setting in the west, the man heard the voice again as tears rolled down his face. In his dream the man heard the voice ask,

"Why are you crying?" The man replied, "I was sick and weak and then that dream gave me a false hope and I have pushed with all that was within me for over 9 months, and that old rock is right where it was when I started."

In his dream, the voice said to him, "I never told you to move the rock, I told you to push against the rock." The man replied, "Yes, Sir, that was the dream." The voice told him to step in front of the mirror and look at himself. As an act of obedience, the man stepped in front of a mirror and looked at himself. The man was amazed. Nine months earlier he had been so sickly and weak, and what he now saw in the mirror was a strong muscular man. The man realized that he had not been coughing all night. The man started thinking of how well he felt for several months and the strength that he had built by pushing on the rock. Then the man realized, that the plan presented in his dream was not for the rock, but for the man.

Have you experienced a life situation that is commonly called caught in a jam; between the devil and the deep blue sea; or between a rock and a hard place? Some have had some hard choices, where you did what you had to do, not what you wanted to do.

In the 2nd Samuel 22:1-4, 47, David reflects on having experienced one difficult situation after another. The prophets wrote, *"David sang to the Lord the words of this song when the Lord delivered him from the hand of all his enemies and the hand of Saul. He said: "The Lord is my rock, my fortress, and my deliverer; my God is my rock, in whom I take refuge, my shield and the horn of my salvation.*

He is my stronghold, my refuge, and my savior—from violent people you save me. 4 "I called to the Lord, who is worthy of praise, and have been saved from my enemies." And in the 47th verse writes, *"The Lord lives! Praise be to my Rock! Exalted be my God, the Rock, my Savior!"*

At the writing of this scripture, David had found himself in one tough situation after another. Saul, king of Israel, because of jealousy had tried to kill him. The Philistines who were the relentless enemies of Israel, had tried to kill him. And David had fallen in love with another man's wife and had the husband killed. He had some tough situations.

Just like David, Christians face some tough times, and some hard situations. We have an enemy who comes after us with but one intention – that's to kill, steal and destroy. But know that when you think that you're between a rock and a hard place, there is a **ROCK** in every hard place. There is a ROCK in every difficult situation. His name is Jesus!

In 2nd Samuel 22: 2 David says, *"The LORD is my **rock**, my fortress and my deliverer; my God is my **rock**, in whom I take refuge, my shield and the horn of my salvation. He is my stronghold, my refuge and my savior—from violent men you save me."*

Rocks have a special significance in the Bible – they represent that which is constant, dependable, durable, firm, lasting, reliable, robust, secure, solid, sound, stable, strong, sturdy, substantial, unmovable, and unyielding.

In the Bible, rocks always point to the Lord. In Isaiah 44:8, God Himself said, *"Do not tremble, do not be afraid. Did I not proclaim this and foretell it long ago? You are my witnesses. Is there any God besides me? No, there is no other Rock; I know not one."*

The Psalmist (18:2) wrote, *"The Lord is my rock, and my fortress, and my deliverer; my God, my strength, in whom I will trust; my buckler, and the horn of my salvation, and my high tower."*

Jesus made it plain in Matthew 7:24-27 that when the world is falling all around us, we need someone in our lives who is solid and unmovable. He talked about a wise man and a foolish man. The foolish man built his home on sand and the wise man built his home on a rock. Storms rose and the floods came to both houses; the rains beat down upon both houses. And, the winds blew against both houses. But it was only the house built upon the rock that was able to stand.

In other words, you need to stand on the Word of God, that Rock, and you'll know what the songwriter meant when he said, "I shall not, I shall not be moved, just like a tree that's planted by the water, I shall not be moved."

David said, "I called to the Lord, who is worthy of praise, and have been saved from my enemies." David tells us that you first have to know that the Lord is a rock in a weary land, shelter in the eye of the storm. Then when you find yourself between a rock and a hard place you have to call on Him. *David said I'm not calling on other kings, not calling on my army, not calling on my friends. I will call upon the Lord."* (2nd Samuel 22:4)

David said I will call upon the Lord because He is the same one who was with me when I fought lions and bears as a shepherd boy. I will call upon the Lord because He is the same one who was with me when I Stood up to a giant with a slingshot and 5 small stones. I will call upon the Lord because He is the same one who was with me when King Saul tried to kill me.

David called on the Lord because, in Him, he found security, peace, and shelter during the storms of life. That's why David said, *"He is worthy to be praised."* (Psalm 145:3)

- If He's been your shelter in the midst of a storm, you know He's worthy to be praised.
- If He's delivered you from a tough situation, you know He's worthy to be praised.
- If He's been your protector, your Jehovah Jireh, you know He's worthy to be praised.
- If He's been your refuge, you know He's worthy to be praised.
- If He's been your sword and your shield, you know He's worthy to be praised.

One songwriter said, "On Christ the solid rock I stand all other ground is sinking sand." Another called Him the Rock of Ages, "cleft for me, let me hide myself in thee." Job said, *"Though He slay me, yet will I trust in Him."* (Job 13:15) David said, *"Yea, though I walk through the valley of the shadow of death, I will fear no evil: for Thou art with me."* (Psalm 23:4)

Paul said, *"We are troubled on every side, yet not distressed; we are perplexed, but not in despair; persecuted, but not forsaken; cast down, but not destroyed."* (2 Corinthians 4:8-9)

He's a rock in a hard place.

Many have gone through storms in life and may wonder if the storms will ever cease. You have faced some heavy pressures, you've had some sleepless nights and you've wept all night long. And just when it seemed like you were getting to your feet something else knocked you down.

Yes, the storms of life just keep on coming. But don't take the presence of the storm that you're going through, to indicate the absence of the Lord.

A preacher once said that if you're going through a financial storm, a health storm, or some other storm that others know about, they can offer you an umbrella, some help. But when you're in the midst of a secret storm. When you are struggling on the inside, torn up emotionally and nobody knows it, you are definitely between a rock and a hard place. You're wondering what to do because you know that God orders your steps, but this day He has ordered trouble.

Let me remind you that just because you're in the will of God, doesn't mean that you won't get in trouble. Job was in the will of God and experienced all kinds of trouble. Lost his family, his possessions, AND his health. Then all his friends showed up and said he must not be living right. But God said that Job was a faithful and upright man who avoided evil. And David was a man after God's own heart. But the truth of the matter is that no matter how faithful we are, we will go through seasons in life when the rain falls, the wind blows and the floods rise.

Ira Tucker of the Dixie Hummingbirds penned the gospel song, "Trouble in My Way" in 1952. He said, "Trouble in my way, I have to cry sometimes. I lay awake at night, but that's alright; Jesus will fix it after a while. Stepped, stepped in the furnace a long time ago; Shadrach, Meshach, and Abednego. No, they were not worried, oh, this I know; They knew that Jesus will fix it after a while."

Whatever you're going through, there is a God who will make a way for you. The battle is not yours, but the Lords. The psalmist said, *"For in the time of trouble he shall hide me in his pavilion: in the secret of his tabernacle shall he hide me; he shall set me up upon a rock."* (Psalms 27:5-8 KJV) That Rock is Jesus and He's worthy to be praised.

∿

In John 16:33 Jesus said, "I have told you these things, so that in me you may have peace. In this world, you will have trouble. But take heart! I have overcome the world." David confirms those words by stating that the Lord has been his rock and his deliverer whenever he was experiencing a life-threatening, difficult situation.

Bottom-line? When you're between a rock and a hard place, there is a ROCK in every hard place. His name is Jesus! He is constant, dependable, durable, firm, lasting, reliable, robust, secure, solid, sound, stable, strong, sturdy, substantial, unmovable and unyielding. So, make sure that you're standing on that solid rock and you'll discover that whatever you're going through, God will make a way for you.

Reflection Questions:

1. What was your last "rock and a hard place" experience? How did you make it through? Would you deal with it differently today as opposed to when it happened?
2. David said in 2 Samuel 22:47 that God deserves all the praise and should be exalted. What can you praise the Lord for, today?

CHAPTER 12

COMMIT TO FOLLOWING JESUS

A young man asked the wise man in his village. "How do I find my purpose?" "Follow me," said the old man. At a river, the sage said, "There are three types of prospectors here. Those who strike gold straight away, others who pan for years before finding gold, and then those individuals who give up after panning for a day, a week, or a year and never finding gold." The young man asked, "What has this to do with finding my purpose?"

The old man smiled and said, "There are those in life who look for their purpose and find it almost immediately. Some others have to look a bit harder, perhaps for many years, but they persist and find it. Finally, some become frustrated with the search and give up too soon, returning to a life of meaningless wandering."

"Can everyone find their purpose?" asked the young man. "Son, there are no guarantees that you will be able to find it quickly, the only guarantee is that if you give up and stop looking for it, you'll never find it." The young man looked despondent, feeling that he had wasted his time with the old man. He felt a reassuring hand on his shoulder, "I can sense your frustration, but let me assure you, if you can find your true calling in life, you will live with passion, make the world a better place, be richer than you could imagine and feel as though the very face of God Himself is smiling upon you. That may happen next week, next year, or in the years ahead, but the search will be worth it and your life will never be the same again. So, for now, your purpose is to find your purpose." (Source Unknown)

A similar conversation is found in Luke 9:57 – 62 (NIV)

"As they were walking along the road, a man said to him (Jesus), "I will follow you wherever you go." Jesus replied, "Foxes have dens and birds have nests, but the Son of Man has no place to lay his head."

He (Jesus) said to another man, "Follow me." But he replied, "Lord, first let me go and bury my father." Jesus said to him, "Let the dead bury their own dead, but you go and proclaim the kingdom of God."

Still another said, "I will follow you, Lord; but first let me go back and say goodbye to my family." Jesus replied, "No one who puts a hand to the plow and looks back is fit for service in the kingdom of God."

Many have sung or at least heard the song, "Where He leads me, I will follow." Truth be told, conversion, and confessing faith is the easy part, committing to follow Jesus is the hard part.

Commitment is a powerful and profound word with many associated words and phrases, all based on the root word, commit. When we commit, we make a decision, not a maybe decision or a wishy-washy decision. We plan to do what we say we will do. We have no option but to do what we have committed to. We don't make or accept excuses; only results. We remain loyal to what we said we were going to do long after the mood we said it in, has passed.

Most people fail, not because of a lack of desire but because of a lack of commitment. Because it is a commitment that transforms a promise into reality. So, if you remember nothing else, remember that Commitment is an act, not a word. And Jesus knows that talk is cheap. This is seen in the encounters between Jesus and three "want to be" disciples. Through these encounters, Jesus makes plain what it means to be committed to following Him.

In Luke 9:57 -58, we see the first encounter as the first man says to Jesus, *"I will follow you wherever you go."* This must be the resolve of all that have made Jesus their choice. But Jesus tells him in verse 58 that, *"Foxes have dens and birds have nests, but the Son of Man has no place to lay his head."*

Saying "I will follow Jesus" is a powerful, profound promise. But Jesus is not looking for promises but commitment. In Matthew 16:24 Jesus says, *"If anyone desires to come after Me, let him deny himself, and take up his cross, and follow Me."*

Make no mistake, the path of righteousness is not an easy one. In Ephesians 6:12 Paul writes *"For our struggle is not against flesh and blood, but against the rulers, against the authorities, against the powers of this dark world and against the spiritual forces of evil in the heavenly realms."*

We also see in Matthew 7:13-14 Jesus telling us that we should *"Enter through the narrow gate. For wide is the gate and broad is the road that leads to destruction, and many enter through it. But small is the gate and narrow the road that leads to life, and only a few find it."*

Jesus is telling the first man who volunteers to follow Him (and us) that we must count the cost to be His disciple. Proclaiming Jesus as Savior is easy but accepting Him as Lord requires that we understand that there will be some things that we have to give up, some habits that we will have to put off, some friends and maybe even some family members that we will have to leave behind.

To follow Jesus requires a commitment, not just involvement. You know the story of the chicken and the pig who decide to provide breakfast for the farmer. The pig said to the chicken, it's easy for you to give up an egg but I have to give all that I have. In other words, the chicken was involved but the pig had to be committed regardless of the cost.

If you are committed you are on call for Jesus 24/7 and will only give God your very best. Commitment to follow Jesus is not a walk with Jesus only when you want to or when it's convenient; it's a walk with Jesus all the time. Commitment means that we are willing to give up our old selves to become the person Christ has created us to be. Paul said in 2 Corinthians 5:17, *"If anyone is in Christ, he is a new creation; old things have passed away; behold, all things have become new."* If you are Committed, what you do for God will always be more than what you do for the world.

Jesus says to another man, "Follow me." But the man replied, "Lord, first let me go and bury my father." What was Jesus' response? "Let the dead bury their own dead, but you go and proclaim the kingdom of God."

Jesus' reply might sound insensitive. It sounded like this man wanted to bury his father. Isn't this a reasonable request? But Jesus knows that it's not a request but an excuse.

Jesus knew that it was unlikely that this man's father had died because that would mean he was in mourning and would not be here with Jesus. Secondly, it would not be in sync with other teachings of the Bible – honor your father and mother. My brothers and sisters, God does not contradict Himself.

Listen to what the man says, "LORD, FIRST let me go..." In other words, Lord, I will follow you on my terms. I have some priorities that are greater than following you. "I have a family to take care of and I cannot follow you right now. Wait until my father **has** died, then I may consider." An excuse.

We have our excuses. But Jesus tells him "to let the dead bury the dead." In other words, Jesus says, trust Me and know that I will take care of you, your parents, and your family. I will take care of you if you put me first. In Matthew 6:33 Jesus said, *"But seek first His kingdom and His righteousness, and all these things will be given to you as well."* And in Matthew 22:37, Jesus says that we are to Love the Lord thy God with all thy heart, mind, and soul.

When Jesus calls you to serve, don't delay and don't make excuses. Jesus wanted him (and us) to know the urgency of making your life count for the Kingdom of God!" Let me remind you that Jesus came to save the world from eternal death. As a child, He understood the urgency when He said, *"I must be about my Father's business."* (Luke 2:49) Likewise, Jesus expects us to go about our business for him with that same sense of urgency – I have to get it done now. I don't have a lot of time. Tomorrow's not promised!

Before His death, Jesus gave us our purpose, our mission. In Matthew 28:19-20 He said, *"Go and make disciples of all nations, baptizing them in the name of the Father and of the Son and the Holy Spirit, and teaching them to obey everything I have commanded you."* We must be careful that we don't place so much focus on our programs, our plans, or our priorities, that we forget our purpose!

75

Finally, in Luke 9:61-62, Jesus gives us the final element that should be part of our Christian commitment. "Still another said, *"I will follow you, Lord; but first let me go back and say good-bye to my family."* Again, on the surface, this looks like a reasonable request. But Jesus knew it was just an excuse and took the opportunity to state another principle that His followers are to take note of. Jesus replied, *"No one who puts his hand to the plow and looks back is fit for service in the Kingdom of God."*

I'm not a farmer but I believe that when you plow, your goal, your purpose is to create straight rows for planting. And to do so, you have to be focused on where you're going, not where you have been.

This third "want-a-be" follower of Christ said, in response to Jesus' call to discipleship, two problematic phrases: first and go back. What do we put first ahead of prayer, bible study, Sunday school, and worship service? What do we put first ahead of the Lord? If you're putting something else first, you're not committed. God has always had a desire for our best. – not your leftovers.

Then there's the phrase, "Go Back." Paul said in Philippians 3:12-14, *"Brethren, I count not myself to have apprehended: but this one thing I do, forgetting those things which are behind, and reaching forth unto those things which are before, I press toward the mark for the prize of the high calling of God in Christ Jesus.*

Committed Christians don't look back because if you look back you may go back to old habits. Our commitment to Jesus is not just an important thing, it is the most important thing in life and it cannot be an emotional decision. The first man who encountered Jesus was probably caught up in the excitement of the big crowd following Jesus, and people getting healed, and he wanted to be a part of it. But if you're not committed, you won't have the faith to carry you through the tough times.

Commitment to Christ cannot be an whenever I can find the time decision either. You can't serve just when it's convenient.

Third, commitment to Christ cannot be a phase in life. I'll serve the Lord for a while. But if things don't work out for me as a Christian, I'll go back into the world. Let me remind you of Lot's wife, who was told not to look back but did anyway and was turned into a pillar of salt. If you're committed to Jesus, turning back, and quitting is not an option.

In the Olympic Games of 1968 the Olympic stadium was packed as the final event, the marathon was ending. The crowd erupts as the first runner, crosses the finish line. Runner after runner enters the stadium and crosses the finish line. Way back in the field was another runner, John Akwha-ri of Tanzania. Only a few people knew that he had fallen and injured his leg and could no longer run but could only hop on one leg. One hour after the winner crossed the finish line, John finished the race. Reporters asked why he didn't give up, he said, "My country did not send me to the Olympics to start the race but to finish the race. I was committed to doing just that."

How many of you are willing to commit to finishing this Christian race? To press toward the mark for the prize of the high calling of God in Christ Jesus. How many are willing to follow Jesus all the way?

Consider the life story of a 19th-century Christian convert of East Indian descent. It is thought that the convert sang this song as he and his family were killed for their faith. He sang . .

"I have decided to follow Jesus; No turning back, no turning back. Tho' none go with me, I still will follow, My cross I'll carry, till I see Jesus; No turning back, No turning back. The world behind me, the cross before me, No turning back, no turning back."

I'm glad Jesus was committed to our salvation and gave His all. I'm glad He marched up Golgotha's Hill, carrying He carried His cross. I'm glad He didn't turn back. I'm glad He gave His best for you and me. And He deserves the best from us. Our best means that we might have to deny ourselves, our preferences, our priorities. Our best means that we're not half-hearted disciples or sometime followers. Our best is to commit to following Jesus, every day!

≈

While God is not looking for perfect people (because there are none), He is looking for committed, faithful people. 1 Corinthians 4:2 clearly states that *"it is required that those who have been given a trust must prove faithful."* So how do you increase or grow your faith? To grow in faith, we must develop at least two habits: The habit of Feeding on the Word of God and the habit of Communing with the Lord. A habit is when you do something so regularly, so repeatedly, that it becomes automatic. You don't have to think about doing the thing anymore.

If you only feed on the Word of God on Sunday, you won't have the strength to fight, the strength to remain encouraged, the strength to withstand the attacks of the devil, the temptations of the flesh, and the attractions of the world. Therefore, if you want to grow your faith, come to Sunday worship, have your personal study time, and come to midweek bible study, and have others that you can discuss the Word with. Then find a place to serve, a place to do, to exercise what we are instructed to do.

The second primary spiritual habit we need to develop is the habit of prayer. Jesus prayed often and taught His disciples to pray. Prayer has to become a habit.

REFLECTION QUESTIONS:

- Examine your commitment and faith today, is it growing?
- Are you on a regular diet of healthy spiritual food?
- Do you have a regular time of private time with the Lord? If not set one and make it a habit.

Milton Keynes UK
Ingram Content Group UK Ltd.
UKHW041041121124
451094UK00002B/247